HISTORIC LAREDO

An Illustrated History of Laredo & Webb County

by María Eugenia Guerra

Published for the Webb County Heritage Foundation

Historical Publishing Network
A division of Lammert Publications, Inc.
San Antonio, Texas

Contents

First Edition

ISBN: 1-893619-16-8

Library of Congress Card Catalog Number: 2001087283

Historic Laredo: An Illustrated History of Laredo & Webb County

author: María Eugenia Guerra
cover artist: Janet Krueger
contributing writer for "sharing the heritage": Sharon Cruz

Historical Publishing Network

president: Ron Lammert
vice president: Barry Black
project representatives: Pat Steele, Roger Smith
director of operations: Charles A. Newton, III
administration: Angela Lake
Donna Mata
graphic production: Colin Hart
John Barr

PRINTED IN SINGAPORE

An old adage tells us that history belongs to those who write it. As a journalist, I have come to know that history belongs to those who inspired it, perhaps to those who had no idea they were, by their acts, being entered into the chronicle of the long and colorful history of this region. That is the history I hope to share here.

I am compelled to note that the significance of the past is weighted by the circumstances of the present, the memories of the teller tempered by the world as it exists today. And finally, I wish to point out that the telling of a story does not necessarily begin at the beginning, and so I offer these stories long after the colonial period, long after the Republic of the Río Grande, and late in this city's growth.

I offer an additional disclaimer—this is not a history compiled academically by a historian. For such a chronicle, I commend you to the excellent work of my esteemed colleagues in education: Dr. Jerry Thompson, Dr. Stanley Green, and Dr. Carlos Cuellar who have done much to collect and tell the early history of this region, individuals who have fostered the goals of the Webb County Heritage Foundation.

Even as a child, one who listened to stories on front porches, I had an idea that this place called Laredo, this city of my heart, was formed by events rich in history, language, and culture. Many decades later, with a look back at the ebb and flow of historical events that occurred in my lifetime, I fashion into print for the purpose of this book, stories of recent history and stories of some of those not-so-long-ago events, those individuals, those times that shaped all our lives all along this border.

María Eugenia Guerra

An assembly of armed Laredoans in a photograph taken in 1892 and labeled "Vigilantes assembled to protect homes from attack by Indians." Pictured from left to right are Jesus Navarro, Pablo Villarreal, Charles Schmidt, Charles Deutz, Raymond Martin, Justo Penn, John Orfila (on the keg), Eligio Yzaguirre, Joe Mas, William Thaison, Abe Moseling, and Richard Tarver.

WEBB COUNTY HERITAGE FOUNDATION

Laredo City Hall complete with the bellfry lost in a 1905 tornado spawned by a hurricane.

WEBB COUNTY HERITAGE FOUNDATION

HISTORY LESSONS

History would not overlook a settlement whose earliest official visitor from the Spanish crown in 1757 was José Tienda de Cuervo, Knight of the Order of Santiago, Captain of Dragoons of the City of Veracruz and Judge Inspector of the Gulf of Mexico.

Our history has been, and is, the history of Spain, Mexico, France, the Republic of Texas, the United States, the Confederacy, and the short-lived Republic of the Río Grande. It is also the history of colonialism, land grants, the displacement of Native Americans, cattle, ranches, the railroad, cotton, coal, onions, oil and gas exploration, and international trade. It is also, unfortunately, the history of environmental disregard for the only source of drinking water for several million Mexicans and Texans.

Ours is a mutual history shared up and down the border region, a vast and lasting history visible in the sandstone block houses built two centuries earlier, in hand-cut curb stones, in the stark, imposing beauty of San Agustín Church, in hitching posts outside old homes.

Our collective history continues most significantly, however, in each of us, for we are ourselves the keepers, the vessels, and the sum totals of our cultural history—who we were as much as who we are now and who we shall become.

History is not static. It moves some moments in small, subtle increments and other times by leaps and lurches; but it is moving, always moving, changing in ways reflected in language, in traditions, and in the collective memory of our region.

Our grandparents thought in Spanish in order to form sentences in English. Some of us now pull our thoughts together in English to stumble through Spanish, mirror-image opposites of who we once were. Are we American? Are we Mexican? Are we Mexican-American? We pose the questions, and one day history answers them.

It was perhaps our proximity to our history and the motherland and the ubiquity of our history in language and on the landscape of South Texas and Northern Mexico that caused it to be omitted altogether from the Texas history lessons we learned in junior high. So pervasive, whole, and obvious to us was our history that it was invisible to those to whom it did not belong. The antics of Ma and Pa Ferguson filled our lessons, not the history of the colonization of this region or the role of the Catholic Church or the Lipan Apaches in the settlement of this area; not the Republic of the Río Grande, not the battle glories of Col. Santos Benavides; not the defeat of the revolutionary Juan Nepomuceno Cortina at Carrizo (formerly Zapata); not the history of the other Spanish colonial settlements that were homes to our ancestors and the springboard for their northern migrations into this country—Guerrero Viejo, Dolores, Ciudad Mier. Not the history of Zapata, San Ygnacio, Los Ojuelos, Falcón, and Palafox. Not the history of the *vaquero* ranching traditions appropriated into myth by the American cowboy.

Whether by design of edict or by uncalculated disregard, our history was edited for us in a less-than-subtle attempt to create distance from our past, perhaps so that we could better assimilate into a nation whose common history had its origins in England and at Plymouth Rock. By the omission and discounted emphasis of our own history, we would learn that real history had happened to other people in other places.

Yet we felt our history, and were as close to it as the stories told in our families, stories we took from the kitchen table, from the ranches, from the *monte*, and from the river *vega*. It was the history we saw in the faces that stared out of old family photos of great-uncles and grandfathers as revolutionaries, family portraits of austere-looking *abuelos* (grandparents) and *vis-abuelos* (great grandparents) whose ancestors left Spain in the 1600s, landed at Veracruz, and moved for centuries through Mexico northward, always northward, braiding their personal histories on the greater tapestry of the history of Mexico. Ours is the history we see in our own faces in the mirror, the history we have heard since birth in *corridos*, language, nursery rhymes, maxims, prayers, and in the ironies of our folk lore.

At this bend in the river, the portals of history swing open wide and both ways over the shared resources of the now environmentally besieged Río Bravo del Norte, a historic place of confluence for the souls of two cities, two cultures, two nations, the future of one fastened to the other. It is here that history pauses to define and re-make itself over a river that never meant to be a border. On both sides of the river, the door swings open one way to reveal the past and the other way to look ahead to the future, to who we

❖

The ranchlands, arroyos, and creek bottoms of Webb County offer up a bounty of points and scrapers from the Catan, Tortugas, Abasolo, and the Matamoros period. Found points, arrow tips, and scrapers, such as those from the Tortugas period, date from 4000 B.C. to 1000 A.D. Others, like the Abasolo, date from 4000 B.C to 500 A.D and into the 18th century.

❖

The coat of arms of José de Escandón, chief colonizer of Nuevo Santander; drawing of Escandón.

WEBB COUNTY HERITAGE FOUNDATION

will become. Our city was—and is—a passage from the old world to the new. Inexplicably, our future lies at both ends of the passage. Surrounded by our collective past and our collective memory of it, we move through the present, a watchful eye on that which is old giving way to the new, ever mindful of what we must keep.

Los primeros, los indígenas

It is the ranchlands that yield some of the most significant clues about the first inhabitants of this part of South Texas. A walk in an arroyo or a look along a place where water drains on the desert floor might produce a beautiful bit of history in a flint tool, an indicator, an historical marker, if you will, for understanding *los indígenas*.

There is a way these objects feel in your hand while you comprehend that you have run your fingers across the technology of hundreds and thousands of years ago—literally the cutting-edge technology of those times. Crude in concept by today's standards, but so beautiful in the detail of the sharp, fluted edges made by the strike of an antler tool, these arrowheads provide an amazing look back at the first residents of this area. It is possible to back-date them several hundred years or several thousand years. Flint knapping was a technology that changed little over time and geographical expanse.

Humans have been living in this part of the world for more than 8,000 years. These earliest inhabitants we now call generally Paleo Indians, because of the time period in which they lived, but we know very little about them. We do know that they lived here in relative peace and comfort for almost seven thousand years before the Spanish came. The irony of that is that they disappeared within 100 years after contact with the Spanish, dying of disease, displacement, and warfare. Euro-Americans have lived along the Rio Grande only 1/9th of the time the area has been inhabited.

The small bands of Indians living here when the Spanish arrived include the Carrizos and the Katuhanos, both of which are generally considered to be part of a larger group of South Texas and Northern Mexico Indians called Coahuiltecans. They were hunter-gatherers who lived in small, autonomous units and made their home wherever food and water was plentiful. Their diet was varied and nutritious, and their appearance reflected their health: tall and handsome by all accounts. For meat, they hunted bison, deer, antelope, javelina, prairie dogs, rabbits, mice, birds, snakes, and insects. They gathered prickly pear, pecans, acorns, *sotol*, *agave*, *maguey* and mesquite beans, which they pulverized into a flour for bread or mashed into a thick gruel. Archeological evidence tells us that food sources were more abundant because the environment was somewhat different one thousand years ago. In prehistoric times, South Texas plains were mostly fertile grasslands, home of much more animal and plant life than at present, and water was also more abundant. The life of a prehistoric South Texas Indian was probably fairly pleasant.

The arrival of the Spanish launched the beginning of the end of thousands of years of Indian occupation of this region. Spanish settlers pushed the Indians out of their favored encampment sites, brought livestock which displaced their wild game, and overgrazed the grasslands. They brought unknown diseases—measles, smallpox, and syphilis—which killed vast numbers of Indians regionally and ultimately decimated the entire Indian population of the Americas. Locally, in skirmish after skirmish, the Spanish killed off or displaced the Coahuiltecans; the displaced were forced to move into Apache or Comanche territory where they were killed in warfare, tolerated, or assimilated by those tribes.

A small number of survivors were taken into various Spanish missions throughout the Southwest. In 1760 two Spanish friars mastered one of the variants of the Coahuiltecan language and wrote a manual for use in administering church rituals. Through this manual, we now know that Coahuiltecans were related to the Hokan language group of California. And in fact, they do resemble a Hokan language group there, the Yuman of Southern California. Perhaps the Coahuiltecans and Yumans represent the remains of an early occupation of the entire southwestern United States thousands of years ago. The group was split by an invasion of stronger migrants pushing south, predecessors of the Hopi, Comanche, Navajo, and Apache, and forced into marginal areas in California, Texas, and Northern Mexico.

In post-Columbian times, the Coahuiltecans were again displaced by other tribes, the Lipan Apache and the Comanche. These great horsemen of the Southern Plains were forced out of their own territory by European encroachment. They led raids into the territory of the Coahuiltecans, forcing out the natives and terrorizing settlers until late in the 19th century.

LOS QUE SIGUIERON: THE COLONIAL SETTLERS

The few remaining old stone buildings of Laredo are of the same vernacular vintage as the sandstone block structures of the abandoned and sometimes partly submerged Spanish colonial townsites of Guerrero Viejo, San Bartolo, old Lopeño, old Falcón, Uribeño, old Ramireño, El Tigre, El Clareño, El Capitaneño, and Tepezán.

Except for Guerrero Viejo, which remains largely intact since its abandonment by condemnation in 1952, the waters of the Falcón reservoir have done much to lay to waste the grandness of the architecture of those small Spanish colonial settlements. Fortunately, much vernacular architecture has been preserved downriver in San Ygnacio and Roma as well as in Ciudad Mier and Ciudad Miguel Alemán.

The richness of architectural detail that survives in these old structures tells a story of the lives of those who built them over 200 years ago and what were their criteria for comfort and survival in so inhospitable a terrain.

It takes but a second to intuit by the precisely square mass of un-mortared sandstone blocks the enduring craftsmanship of the early builders. A longer look at the whole of a stone wall with its dry-stacked arches, cypress lintels over doors and windows, and *troneras* (gun ports) bears out the intended permanence of the homes, homes meant to offer enduring shelter and formidable protection. The durable aesthetics of those old buildings with their elegant, hand-forged hardware of ancient doors allow, too, a look into the character of those builders, those owners who meant to stay. There is a refrain to the contemplation of function fused with the beauty of those old structures: *with their hands*.

It is not difficult to find the few surviving old sandstone block buildings left in Laredo, those remaining after the city gave up many of its architectural treasures to the construction of the Juárez Lincoln International Bridge through the heart of one of its oldest and most historically rich neighborhoods, El Azteca. You have only to walk along Zaragoza Street at the river's edge to view some excellent examples of the architecture of the early residents of this region. Between the Juárez Lincoln Bridge and International Bridge I, you will come across the Agustín Vidaurri Home, now the American Legion building (809 Zaragoza); the Lockwood Customs brokerage house (819 Zaragoza); or the Bartolomé García Home, once the capital building of the Republic of the Río Grande and now the Republic of the Río Grande Museum (1000 Zaragoza).

❖

The drystacked (now razed and lost) wall of sandstone block of the Margarito Sanchez home in downtown Laredo.

WEBB COUNTY HERITAGE FOUNDATION

Author Andres Tijerina characterizes early ranching in South Texas as a system of defensive settlement that the Spaniards had used for a thousand years in Spain and in the New World.

Tijerina's *Tejano Empire* is a concise narrative for the lives of those early settlers, a valuable resource that gives the names and explanations for the objects, customs, and ranch traditions of the colonial settlers. Tijerina provides a wealth of detail for the *casas de sillar* (quarried block houses), what grew in the gardens of those homes, how they worked their livestock, what they wore, and the objects that filled their homes.

That narrative, coupled perhaps with a walk through the ruins of Guerrero Viejo or the narrative of an *abuelo* (grandfather) allows a picture of cultured, genteel ranching families making their lives on this edge of the Chihuahuan Desert.

Who were those people and what were their names? What fire of soul and spirit pointed the compass of their hearts north from the center of Mexico? Who were those first colonial settlers, adventurous and intrepid sons and daughters of those who had sailed Spanish ships to step onto Mexican soil at Veracruz or Panuco in the 1600s? Who were they, those who for the next century-and-a-half would move north to Mexico City, Monterrey, and Revilla and the other border settlements and *ranchos* that became a springboard for José De Escandón's colonization of the Spanish province of Nuevo Santander on both banks of the Río Bravo del Norte?

Like many other residents of this region, I can chart on a globe the who, what, when, where, why,

❖

As late as 1922 barrileros *in donkey-drawn carts delivered river water to Laredo homes.*

WEBB COUNTY HERITAGE FOUNDATION

and how of us from the 1600s to the present in South Texas. With minor variations of geography, and within decades, the story of my family mirrors the story of many who share the same ancestral ties of culture, history, language, and tradition.

When in 1685 the Spanish explorer Alonso de León passed through what is now the northwest corner of Webb County, the first of Laredo's ancestors had been born in the New World. De León, scouting for the reported presence of the French in the area, followed the Río Grande to the Gulf Coast and then headed southward. Persistent in his search for the French, he would return to cross the Río Grande on two other occasions.

ESCANDÓN'S *NUEVO SANTANDER*

When another Spaniard, Miguel De la Garza Falcón, traveled in 1747 through this river region from the upriver settlement of Mission San Juan Bautista and east along the northern bank of the Río Grande, Guerra Cañamars had begun their northward migration in earnest across Mexico. De la Garza Falcón led one of seven military columns moving to meet chief colonizer Captain General José de Escandón at the mouth of the Río Grande. Escandón gathered information, records, and journals from his captains who detailed the geography and water sources of the vast region as well as a census of indigenous populations. Basing himself on the data he had harvested for the area, Escandón reported to the Viceroy at Querétaro that there were sites for 14 proposed *villas* in Nuevo Santander. He also requested funding of 58,000 pesos.

The first settlement was established at Villa de Santa Ana de Camargo on March 6, 1749. The second settlement was founded on March 19, 1749 at Nuestra Señora de Guadalupe de Reynosa, which was 12 leagues downriver from Camargo.

The third settlement, which was organized and led by Vicente Guerra Cañamar, was at the juncture of the Río Salado and the Río Grande. It was called Villa de San Ignacio de Revilla, later called Guerrero. Twenty-six families joined Guerra Cañamar to settle there in May of 1750, their earliest actions setting the stage for a great part of the rich cultural history of northern Mexico and South Texas.

Nuestra Señora de los Dolores, eight leagues from Revilla and 30 leagues downriver from San Juan Bautista, was established on the north bank of the Río Grande in 1750 by Coahuila rancher José Vasquez Borrego.

Escandón ended up establishing 13 settlements at twice the cost he had been allocated by the Viceroy. Despite an early period of flourishing and increasing inventories of horses and cattle, the village of Dolores fell prey perhaps as much to hostile Indian attacks as to a social structure that resembled a medieval fiefdom. Dolores Nuevo was established a mile upriver high on the river bluff. Two other ranches, Corralitos and Hacienda de San Ygnacio, were also settled. The settlement of Refugio was founded in 1796, and was re-named Matamoros in 1824.

THE *RANCHO* OF LAREDO

With Escandón's blessing, Tomás Sánchez, a rancher who lived across the river from the Dolores settlement, established the *rancho* of Laredo on May 15, 1755 at a ford in the river built earlier by the Spanish officer Jacinto De León, a spot called El Paso de Jacinto and later, El Paso de los Indios. The *rancho* of Laredo, which established on 15 leagues of land, grew from the three settling families to 85 inhabitants by 1757. In 1767, Laredo recorded 185 residents. In that same year, a General Visit of the Royal Commission to the Colonies of Nuevo Santander assigned land grants to families that had settled the area. Land was designated in three categories: land for grazing, land which would be irrigated, and the six leagues which would form the town proper. The Commission also set out the method for surveying the town's public plaza and for setting aside land for public buildings and the church. The commission determined the width of 89 *porciones* (land grants) that were granted on lands adjacent to the townsite of Laredo.

In 1798, Laredo counted 708 residents, including Carrizo Indians. By 1828, the town's population had reached 2,052.

The ranches of the vast grazing lands along the border fueled the economy of the towns that the early *villas* of Nuevo Santander had become and gave birth to the cattle industry and to the *vaquero* whose ranching practices and rich traditions were later appropriated by the American cowboy.

The first half of the 1800s wrought significant changes to the *frontera* town of Laredo, which was poised at the northernmost edge of the Spanish colonial and Mexican frontier. For the most part, however, Laredo would remain removed from the armed frays of two struggles for independence—Mexico's from Spain and then Texas' from Mexico. While Laredo sat out various incursions, battles, and expeditions over the first half of the century, it would become engaged in the establishment of the Republic of the Río Grande and in the Civil War.

Resistance to the Crown

Resistance to the Spanish crown brought the movement of armed troops to and through Laredo. Spanish Royalist troops quartered in Laredo in 1813, sought to end a Republican rebellion led by Bernardo Gutiérrez de Lara of Revilla and others across the territory. Royalist resistance ended with Mexican independence in 1821 and in the swell of name-changing that followed independence, the Spanish province of Nuevo Santander became the Mexican state of Tamaulipas, the downriver town of Revilla became Ciuidad Guerrero.

It was Indian attacks and not revolution that greatly preoccupied the citizenry of Laredo. In the political disarray following Mexican Independence and in the disappearance of the implied safety of Royalist *presidios*, Laredo and other *frontera* towns faced fierce repeated Comanche attacks. Preoccupied with the safety of the lives of their families and the sizeable livestock holdings that had made them economically independent from Mexico City, displeased with the ineffectual, unresponsive Centralist Mexican government's failure to provide for the defense of the region, Laredoans also looked askance at the rumblings of the Anglo Tejanos seeking separation from Mexico.

The Republic of the Río Grande

The conditions of those perilous years on the *frontera* proved fertile ground for the formation of the northern confederation of the Republic of the Río Grande, a brief though dramatic chapter in the history of the region that officially began with a November 5, 1838 *pronunciamento* in Guerrero in opposition to the Centralist government and a call for a return to the Mexican Constitution of 1824. At a January 1, 1840 convention at Oreveña Ranch near Carrizo (Zapata), ranchers and representatives of the Mexican states of Nuevo Leon, Coahuila, and Tamaulipas formed the Republic of the Río Grande and named Laredo its capital city. The new government's legislative council of eight delegates remained in Guerrero to have access to a press which printed the official Federalist newspaper, *Correo del Río Bravo del Norte*.

History professor Dr. Jerry Thompson writes that the inspired hero of that fated and short-fused resistance to the distant and unresponsive Centralist government of Mexico was Col. Antonio Zapata, a bravehearted *guerrerense* who had earned the respect and loyal following of those who knew him as a courageous Indian fighter. Disorganized from the top down, the revolutionary forces were led by the timid, hesitant commander-in-chief Antonio Canales who was unable to command troops effectively, or even to raise them. The revolutionists lost the capital city of the Republic of the Río Grande when General Arista marched Centralist troops into Laredo and took it.

The revolutionary army was outmatched by the Centralist army at Santa Rita de Morelos in a March 24 battle during which Col. Zapata was captured. Canales, bungling a rescue effort, was late in reaching Zapata, who repeatedly declined a pardon in exchange for joining the Centralist forces. He was court martialed, executed, and beheaded five days after his defeat. Antonio Zapata died, M.B. Lamar wrote, "a martyr to his fidelity and his patriotism."

Despite the defeat of its most significant and venerated hero, and probably its true leader, the Republic of the Río Grande persisted with resistance to the Centralist government of Mexico and managed to recapture its capital city.

The army of the Republic of the Río Grande met decisive defeat at Saltillo. The terms of surrender of the revolutionary forces were completed on November 6, 1840 on the northern banks of the Río Grande opposite Camargo.

[The brief history of the Republic of the Río Grande is well-documented by Texas A&M

This panoramic photograph of an encampment at Ft. McIntosh was taken around 1924.

WEBB COUNTY HERITAGE FOUNDATION

International University historian Dr. Jerry Thompson in *Historic Laredo* and in other of his writings, as well as in Dr. Stan Green's Monograph No. 8: *Laredo, Antonio Zapata, & The Republic of the Río Grande*.]

The Battle for Texas

With the revolutionary forces defeated, the Centralist government of Mexico renewed its efforts to regain Texas. General Rafael Vasquez led an army of 400 Mexican soldiers across the Río Grande above Laredo and moved to enter San Antonio. A column of 130 soldiers under Lt. Col. Ramon Valera crossed at Mier and took Goliad and Refugio.

Four-hundred Texans prepared for an expedition against Matamoros and were met at a bend in the Nueces River by now-Centralist devotee Antonio Canales, former commander of the army of the Republic of the Río Grande. Canales claimed victory at Matamoros. An army of Centralist troops commanded by General Adrian Woll took San Antonio and flew the Mexican flag over the city.

In November of 1842, Laredoans were unwilling hosts to about 1,200 Texans of the Southwestern Army of Operations led by General Alexander Somervell, an outfit that finds its name in history as the Mier Expedition. The Texans, in preparation for pursuit of the Mexican army, wanted food and clothing. To the displeasure of the oppressive visitors, Laredoans had secreted away many of the town's stores and surpluses. Though they camped south of Laredo where Chacón Creek and the Río Grande converge, angry troops returned to Laredo to sack the town, helping themselves to the contents of stores and buildings that they entered by force.

Enroute to Dolores and San Ygnacio, some of the Texans broke from the ranks and headed back home. The rest pressed toward Guerrero. An advance party of the Texans met the Mexican army led by Antonio Canales. Fearing a trap, the timorous Canales did not engage the Texans.

Guerrerenses offered the army five days' rations. Somervell refused to allow his men to enter the city and issued an order calling on the army to return to Texas. The majority of the troops refused to return and struck mutiny. About 200 did return to Texas and the remaining troops selected William S. Fisher their new leader.

Oblivious that a large contingent of the Mexican army moved toward them, the Texans moved along the north bank of the river toward Mier. The Texans issued a levy for supplies from the residents of Mier. The armies of Canales and General Ampudia joined forces at Mier and took the goods that had been prepared for the Texans.

The Texans fought to take the plaza of the town and found that they were up against a formidable Mexican army. When the battle of Mier was over, the Texans had surrendered and become prisoners of the Mexican army. They were marched downriver to Matamoros and then to Saltillo and San Luis Potosí. Near Salado, the Texans made a break. Only four made it back to Texas, and the rest were captured or gave themselves up. Santa Anna ordered up his famous black bean lottery to see who would be spared and who would face the firing squad. Those who survived became members of a work gang on a road near Mexico City. they were later sent to a prison in Veracruz. Some of the Texans died and some managed to escape. The

remaining 110 Texans were returned to Texas in late 1844.

When Texas ceased to be a republic and became a state in 1846, the United States recognized its new state's claim to the Río Grande. Mexico, which had recognized the Republic of Texas, broke diplomatic ties with the United States and prepared for war in earnest. The deciding battles of the Mexican-American War, led by General Zachary Taylor, were waged at Palo Alto and at Resaca de la Palma. Other battles followed in 1846 and early 1847, battles fought on Mexican soil and in which the Mexicans yielded Monterrey, Buena Vista, and Mexico City.

The Treaty of Guadalupe Hidalgo was signed by both countries in February of 1848, defining the Río Grande and not the Nueces River as the official border between the two countries. The United States paid Mexico $15 million for 530,000 square miles of California, New Mexico, Nevada, Utah, most of Arizona and parts of Colorado and Wyoming.

According to Dr. Stan Green, the census of 1850 reflected a decline in Laredo's population, as some Laredoans had left to establish Nuevo Laredo across the river. That census also revealed a significant number of non-Hispanic immigrants, mainly Anglo-Americans.

In an effort to secure the nation's border with Mexico, in the years after the signing of the Treaty of Guadalupe Hidalgo, the U.S. Army constructed several military forts along the *frontera*, including Ft. Ringgold at Río Grande City, Ft. Crawford (later Ft. McIntosh) at Laredo, and Ft. Duncan at Eagle Pass.

The history of Ft. McIntosh figures largely in the history of Laredo. A military presence in Laredo provided a measure of stability against Comanche and Lipan Apache raids in the region. The fort was abandoned by the Union Army during the Civil War and was later occupied by the Confederacy. Federal soldiers returned to Ft. McIntosh in 1865 and began permanent construction at the site in 1868. The City of Laredo ceded 208 acres to the federal government in 1875 for further development of the facility. The old fort became the home of Laredo Junior College, which was established in 1946.

The Civil War

Though slavery was not a wholesale practice along the border region, Texas counties on the border overwhelmingly supported secession from the Union in 1861. The residents of Zapata and Webb counties, as did voters in approval across the state, voted in favor 212 to 0 and 62 to 10, respectively, to support the secessionist ordinance presented by the Texas Secession Convention which had met in Austin.

All military posts in the state were turned over to agents of the state. A contingent of 40 armed Tejano Unionists, led by Antonio Ochoa, marched on Carrizo, the Zapata County seat, to prevent officials from taking the Confederate oath of allegiance. They were dissuaded by County Judge Isidro Vela. A Confederate company of 22 riders from Laredo commanded by Captain Matthew Nolan rode into Carrizo and onto El Clareño Ranch where the Unionists were said to be headquartered downriver of Carrizo.

An all-out attack ensued as the Unionists were in the process of surrendering. Nine were killed. Ochoa, who was reportedly in Guerrero, joined the

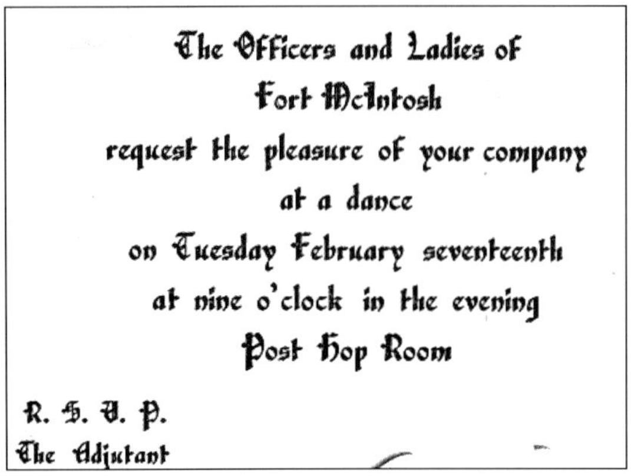

The Officers and Ladies of
Fort McIntosh
request the pleasure of your company
at a dance
on Tuesday February seventeenth
at nine o'clock in the evening
Post Hop Room

R. S. V. P.
The Adjutant

Top: Two spans of the International Bridge on the Mexican side of the river collapsed in 1905 after being hit by a tornado.

WEBB COUNTY HERITAGE FOUNDATION

Above: The Adjutant of Fort McIntosh issued this invitation to a dance hosted by "the Officers and Ladies" of the military fort.

ARTURO DOMINGUEZ

retired border raider Juan Cortina as news spread along the river of the massacre of the Tejano Unionists. Roma and Carrizo braced themselves for a visit from armed forces led by Cortina and the avenging Ochoa who had recruited those residents of Guerrero who wanted satisfaction and justice for the death of their relatives at El Clareño. Confederate Captain Santos Benavides of Laredo offered Carrizo protection, moving onto the ranch of Zapata County boss Henry Raymond with 30 soldiers.

Cortina surrounded the Confederates on May 21 and held them at bay. Captain Refugio Benavides, Santos' brother, made it through from the Mexican side of the river with the news that relief was en route from Laredo. Basilio Benavides and Lt. Charles Callaghan and 33 reinforcements made the 60-mile ride from Laredo to Carrizo (Zapata) in 13 hours. The Benavides brothers engaged Cortina and 70 of his followers in a bitter and violent fight outside of Carrizo. Cortina and many of his men escaped into Mexico.

Zapata and Starr counties were the setting for some of the most dramatic events between the Union loyalists and the Confederates. Union loyalist Octaviano Zapata and his guerrillas attacked a Confederate supply train in Roma in early December of 1862. On December 26 at the Rancho Soledad, the guerrillas killed all but one teamster driving a three-wagon supply train moving from Fort Brown to Ringgold Barracks. Confederate soldiers retaliated by burning 16 mesquite *jacales* to the ground at Rancho Soledad.

Zapata and 200 loyalists rode to El Clareño Ranch, the home of Zapata County Judge Isidro Vela and hanged him in front of his wife and children.

As Octaviano Zapata continued to persist in raids across the border, Captain Refugio Benavides pursued him in Mexico, tracking him near Camargo. Zapata inspired the ire of the Mexican army as well, ambushing troops on the road from Guerrero to Mier. Major Santos Benavides crossed the Río Grande into Mexico below Carrizo and located Zapata's camp. Zapata and many of the insurgents were killed by the Confederates.

The arrival of about 7,000 federalist troops to the border prompted the Confederacy's abandonment of Brownsville.

A Union regiment of 200 soldiers led by Major Alfred E. Holt moved upriver from Brownsville to Laredo to destroy 500 bales of Confederate cotton under the watch of Colonel Santos Benavides. Benavides and 42 Confederate soldiers lay in wait for Holt's regiment on the banks of Zacate Creek, repelling them and forcing their return to Brownsville without every seeing the cotton stacked downtown in San Agustín Plaza.

The sight of armed men at the ready for confrontation or combat continued to be commonplace for the border for the rest of the 19th century and the early part of the next century.

Mexico's bloody grapple with the French armies of the Emperor Napoleon III played itself out in episodes of vicious guerrilla warfare all along the border. The French took Matamoros in 1864, but gave it up in 1866 when 400 Imperialist troops were captured by an Army of Mexican nationalists at the Battle of Santa Gertrudis downriver from Camargo. French rule in Mexico came to an end in June of 1867 with the execution of the Emperor Maximilian.

The raids of cattle thieves, including those of the infamous Juan Cortina who came out of retirement, continued through the late 1890s.

Ranching, the Railroad, Onions

In many respects, the wars and battles of the post-colonial period had been good for the border's economy. The Civil War with its heavy movement of cotton and supplies had been very good for economic development and for the the shipping of goods by steamboats that moved upriver from the coast. The Civil War was especially good to the cattle ranching business. There were reportedly only 3,000 cattle in Webb County in 1859, but the figure leaped to 30,000 by the close of the Civil War.

The sheep industry and the sale of wool had long been a mainstay of the economy of the Río Grande plains and remained so until the last decade of the century. Sheep populations and revenues from wool built steadily from the middle of the century—there were reportedly 3.5 million sheep in the region by 1885, wool selling at a premium of 25¢ per pound. By the end of the century—the once lush plains of the borderlands now overgrazed—sheep raising was in decline.

It was the arrival of the railroad in 1881 to South Texas that brought about the greatest of economic and social changes for Laredo and Webb County. The infusion of new jobs for the railroad builders of the line that would become the Texas Mexican Railway, the shipment of beeves and agricultural products by rail, and the ability to secure manufactured goods from the East Coast changed the way business was conducted in Laredo and began to define the city's potential as a mover of cargo and goods into Mexico.

Towns grew up all along the Texas Mexican Railway line, including Aguilares, Oilton, Mirando City, Bruni, and Peña (Hebbronville). The railroad became the backbone of the cannel coal mining industry which operated mines upriver at San José, Carbon, Darwin, Islitas, and Joyce.

Railroad spurs and the movement of cattle by rail allowed ranching to develop in unprecedented fashion as better markets became more accessible and less labor intensive.

The completion on December 15, 1881 of the standard-gauge International and Great Northern Railroad linked San Antonio and Laredo, further defining Laredo's importance as the crossing point for American goods and materials entering Mexico for further distribution across the country for mining, agriculture, and manufacturing.

In 1890, Webb County recorded 791,000 acres in ranching and farming operations. There were 408 farms in agricultural production in the county in 1900.

The railroads brought a significant influx of Anglo-Americans into the population mix of Webb County and Laredo, and by 1900, they made up a quarter of the recorded population of 21,851. Some of the Anglo immigrants had a penchant for turning rangeland into farmland and relied on pumps to irrigate crops. Thomas Nye's strides in Bermuda Onion production gained attention as Webb County became known as the "Bermuda Capital of the World." In 1910, a record 1,700 rail cars of Bermuda Onions were shipped out of Webb County.

The Mexican Revolution brought new strife and a new wash of blood to the border region after the death of President Francisco Madero in 1913. Laredoans watched the fray firsthand from the riverbanks as Carranzista forces attacked Nuevo Laredo on January 1, 1914. The Mexican Revolution

❖

Above: A Laredo street scene down Flores Avenue reveals the offices of the Laredo Daily Times, G. A. Stowers Furniture on the right, and City Hall down a block and on the left.

WEBB COUNTY HERITAGE FOUNDATION

Below: The view from the Mexican banks of the river circa 1900. The three-story Ursuline Convent and the first International Bridge dominate the picture.

DR. JERRY THOMPSON

❖

Above: Another view down Flores Avenue shows off the facade of the City Hall Building on the 500 block facing the old Strand Theatre and Reed's Drug Store. Note the city's transit system.

WEBB COUNTY HERITAGE FOUNDATION

Below: This May 1911 letter on Webb County letterhead from Sheriff Amador Sanchez recommends Miguel Rodriguez for employment, endorsing him as a well-known, hard-working, and intelligent Laredoan.

ARTURO DOMINGUEZ

pushed through the sieve of the border a steady pulse of Mexicans relocating in the United States.

National guardsmen were called to duty and stationed at the border posts of Fort Brown, Port Isabel, Ringgold Barracks, and Ft. McIntosh. Many remained on the border until the outbreak of World War I in Europe.

Farming production prospered and diversified. Cotton became a cash crop grown on the rich tracts adjacent to the river. A favorable climate, the accessibility of water, and the technology to move water sustained farming in Webb County until the 1930s when agriculture bowed to the economic blows of the Great Depression, market price declines due to competition from the Lower Río Grande Valley, and a rise in the price of diesel which was used to fuel run irrigation pumps at the river's edge.

The Wildcatter's Strike

Wildcatter O.W. Killam's first oil well in the Schott Field south of Mirando City in 1921 began an oil boom of significant importance to the region, setting the table for an industry that would for the rest of the century have measurable impact on the economy of the area and on the tax bases of school districts that would educate the children of Laredo and Webb County. Killam's Schott No. 2 made history with its production of 300-400 barrels of oil per day plus several million cubic feet of natural gas.

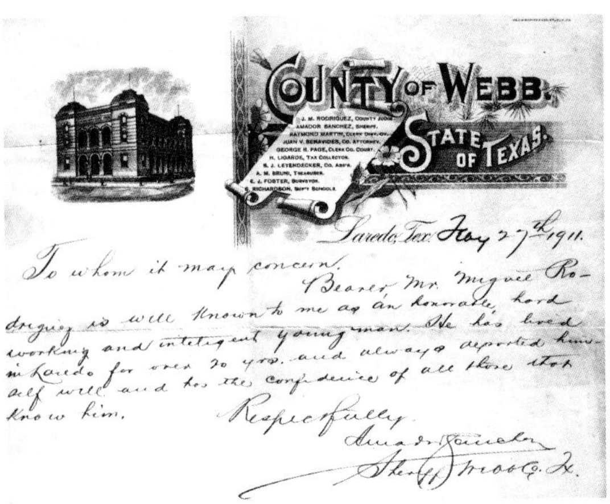

COUNTY OF WEBB. STATE OF TEXAS.

J. M. RODRIGUEZ, COUNTY JUDGE
AMADOR SANCHEZ, SHERIFF.
RAYMOND MARTIN, CLERK DIST. CT.
JUAN V. BENAVIDES, CO. ATTORNEY.
GEORGE R. PAGE, CLERK CO. COURT.
H. LIGARDE, TAX COLLECTOR.
R. J. LEYENDECKER, CO. ASS'R.
A. M. BRUNI, TREASURER.
E. J. FOSTER, SURVEYOR.
RICHARDSON, SUP'T SCHOOLS.

Laredo, Tex. May 27th 1911.

To whom it may concern.

Bearer, Mr. Miguel Rodriguez is well known to me as an honorable, hard working and intelligent young man. He has lived in Laredo for over 30 yrs. and always deported himself well and has the confidence of all those that know him.

Respectfully,

Amador Sanchez

Sheriff Webb Co. Tx.

A native of Missouri and an 1898 graduate of the University of Missouri Law Department, Killam also established the Texpata Pipeline Co. to carry oil to tank farms and to railroad tank cars.

In those days of wooden derricks, O.W. Killam wrote in literature produced to entice investors in the oil field at Mirando, "The drilling is easy. The time required to complete a well is but a few days and the cost is small, ranging from four to eight thousand dollars per well.... The oil is a light fluid, twenty-three gravity, very high in lubricating value. It is found in a 28-foot bed of coarse sandy marl at the top of 300 feet of very rich lignitic carbonaceous deposits in the mid-Yegua, and the wells should last for many years. This geological area is some sixty miles long North and South and several miles wide East and West."

Waxing literary, and probably having a great appreciation for the landscape of South Texas, Killam elaborated on the meaning of "Mirando," telling prospective investors, "Mirando is a gerundive form of the Latin verb 'mirar,' meaning 'to wonder at,' and literally translated means 'deserving to be wondered at' or 'must be wondered at.' In one word, it may be well translated 'marvelous.'"

Seventy-nine years after he wrote this piece, Killam's enticements to investors still sound energetic and full of promise and substance. "It takes people and money to build a town and develop an oil territory," he wrote.

Laredo Air Force Base

The April 17, 1973 decision by the U.S. Department of Defense to close Laredo Air Force Base, an installation that steadily and generously fueled the local economy for over 25 years, packed a resounding wallop to the City's economy, removing about $13 million from the flow of cash through the city.

The 2,000 acre facility on U.S. Hwy. 59 had begun operations in November 1942 as Laredo Army Air Field, which included a gunnery range. The base became inactive in 1945 and the property reverted to the city which used part of the facility as a municipal airport. In 1952, the base was reactivated as Laredo Air Force Base for basic flight training.

The $34.3 million federal investment in the air base (excluding land) dropped $13 million a year into the local economy. Military personnel took home $4.1 million in pay. Civilians took home $3.9 million. Living allowances for military personnel totaled $2 million. Contractor salaries were $1 million. Commissary purchases totaled about $760,000, and other miscellaneous expenses totaled about $500,000. It was estimated that an additional 1,500 service-related jobs in the community were affected by the base closure. Most of the base's 500 civil service employees were being paid well over 1973's minimum hourly wage of $2.90.

Unemployment in Laredo at the time of the base closure in September 1973 was 10.4%. In January of 1974, the figure rose to 18.5%, a figure factored down slightly by 3 or 4% to arrive at a number directly due to the base's closure.

A July 1974 assessment of the economic impact of the base closure was authored by Albert Rodriguez and Jerry Heare of the Texas Industrial Council. The report and its findings, funded by a grant from the Economic Development Administration (EDA), was submitted to The Opportunity Laredo Committee, a committee of citizens who explored options for the re-use and further development of the air base facility. The Department of Defense's Department of Economic Adjustment participated, along with city leaders and business owners, in formulating an initial plan to make best use of the LAFB property once the General Services Administration returned the property to the City of Laredo.

At the time the report was drafted, the population of Laredo was 75,000. Nuevo Laredo's was 180,000. The two cities would be connected by a second international bridge, according to the study's report, with construction scheduled to begin "as soon as the final authorization is provided by the U.S. Coast Guard, which is imminent."

Two other studies were conducted concurrent to the EDA-funded report. One was the Airport Master Plan study funded by the Federal Aviation Agency to define "aeoronautical-related developments at the base" and the other was an additional EDA grant to assess industrial possibilities relative to "the street and road network around the base."

Despite the closure of the base, other aspects of the city's financial network appeared to be thriving. By July 1974, local bank assets had increased by $53 milliion, a 26% increase over the 12 months prior. "All four banks have major building projects underway," the report stated. Sales tax receipts for FY 1974 were being estimated at $1.7 million. Business activity had seen a 15% increase, according to the study, and natural gas reserves in the area were estimated at a trillion cubic feet.

International Trade

Even the most cursory of looks at trade figures for the last decades spell out the vitality of international trade, which has always been the business of Laredo. In the larger scheme of things, the *peso* devaluations of the past have packed punches that changed fortunes and lives, but on the continuum of the history of business on the border, the economic downturns were but hurdles at which the local economy paused briefly and then reconnoitered, re-styled itself, and moved forward.

That has been the story of this place called Laredo. Throughout its history, throughout whichever of the battles for independence touched this city over a century, through natural disasters like floods or other economic downturns like the closure of Laredo Air Force Base in 1973, this has been a city that re-groups, finds its heart, and moves forward.

The last 20 years have made history in the arena of international trade between Laredo and Mexico. The exponential numbers for growth rates fairly sing in superlatives. Between 1980 and 1990, U.S.-Mexico trade grew by 107%. From 1990 to 2000, it grew by another 257%. The number of cross-border loaded trucks increased from 1980 to 1990 by 105%, and between 1990 and 2000, the figure increased by 287%. Rail car crossings increased 97% between 1980 and 1990, and in the decade between 1990 and 2000, it increased by 192%. Business telephone connections grew by

Airmen and officers of Laredo Air Force Base moved over 125,000 pounds of food into Laredo during Hurricane Beulah, one of the most fearsome and devastating hurricanes to move inland. This photograph was taken on September 22, 1963.

WEBB COUNTY HERITAGE FOUNDATION

100% from 1980 to 1990 and another 171% between 1990 and 2000. Building permits from 1980 to 1990 rose by 98%, and 127% between 1990 and 2000. The city's population increased by 34% between 1980 and 1990, and 55% between 1990 and 2000.

The actual numbers are staggering. In 1980, U.S. Mexico trade tallied in the vicinity of $28 billion. By 1990, the figure had climbed to $58 billion. In 1999, it was $197 billion. It is estimated that 2000 will see $207 billion.

According to the Laredo Development Foundation, the ascent in trade began in earnest in 1987 when the twin plant *maquila* industry got its second wind, as both the U.S. and Mexico entered the General Agreement on Tariffs and Trade (GATT) and then the North American Trade Agreement (NAFTA), all of which have fomented growth in the transportation and logistics industry and in the economies of Laredo and Nuevo Laredo.

The twin city *maquiladoras*, the 1960s brainchild of the Mexican government's Border Industrialization Program, were invented to attract foreign capital to Mexico. The establishment and success of plants began a steady stream of growth in the economies of twin cities along the border, streams of profits quite nearly commensurate, some environmentalists say, to the plumes of chemical waste and raw sewage that have degraded the foremost natural resource of the region, the Río Grande. The filth of the river, from which both Laredo and Nuevo Laredo draw its drinking water, has become part of the equation of growth on a border that obeys neither the environmental laws of Mexico nor the United States, Tamaulipas or Texas, Nuevo Laredo or Laredo.

The word infrastructure has become the buzzword of the NAFTA-inspired growth trajectory, a word uttered as much by visiting politicians making promises, as by those local politicians who hold public office and travel to Washington to ask for some more.

While Laredoans in general do not dispute the benefits of the steady wave of economic growth fueled by international trade—it is indisputable—there are some not-so-dazzled by infrastructure, especially that acquired at the expense of environmental concerns or that chosen over dealing with quality of life issues like cleaning the life- sustaining waters of the Río Grande.

Reading through some of the findings of the Rodriguez/Heare EDA study about the closure of Laredo Air Force Base in 1973, one might observe with a subtle mix of sadness and alarm that some things remain as true today as years ago. They wrote, "Laredo is characterized by its social and economic paradoxes. Its flourishing international trade actvity and unusual volume of retail trade, plus the steady stream of Mexico-bound tourists belies the severe urban problems related to outmoded public facilities, street paving, and traffic congestion, and a high poverty level."

James W. Falvella, a writer for the *Laredo Times* in and around 1916, wrote of "the bravest of the brave" and of Laredoans who were making this city a more prosperous and progressive place. The pages of Falvella's beautiful little *Souvenir Album of Laredo, the Gateway to Mexico*—complemented by the photographs of renown Laredo photographer José García—fairly drip with the opportunity and adventure that were the hallmark of those times on this border. Falvella's writing describes the history of settlement of this area, sort of a potpourri amalgam of basic fact stretched to its farthest possibility: "wagon trains over the undulating prairies or the chaparral lands, of how, endangered by the lurking savage behind some huge boulder....or being ambuscaded they were compelled to show that mettle of which the men and women of the early days were possessed in full quantity."

Largely Anglo in his perspectives on a city so peopled by Mexicans, Falvella called our architecture "monotonous one story, square built, flat roof stone or concrete building," and he said that in 1881, there "was not an American built building of modern architecture and design."

The freshness and enthusiasm of his writing and the overall presentation of the little book, however, compensate for his historical transgressions and his failure to recognize that it was seven and not six flags that flew over Laredo.

Oh, but to stand at the river's edge today with Falvella, to be free for a moment of the cacaphony of claxons, air brakes, and the grind of international traffic moving from the heart of one city into another, to believe as Falvella did then of those enterprising and promising times in Laredo, "She has been fortunate in that her destinies were directed by men of integrity and conservation."

Journalists

Los Idar

Old issues of *La Crónica*, which was published in Laredo in the first decade of the 1900s by the Nicasio Idar family reveal a little newspaper with a mind, a heart, and a soul, a Spanish language newspaper unafraid to speak to the social issues of the day, a champion of the well-being and progress of Mexicans living in Texas.

Nicaso Idar and his children Jovita (Jr.), Eduardo, and Clemente Nicasio championed the civil rights and equality issues of Mexican-Texans and voiced the necessity of reversing the perceptible loss of the Mexican culture and the Spanish language. The paper spoke out against discrimination leveled at Mexicans, particularly in the area of education. It also addressed racial hatred and brutality against Mexicans by Anglo-Texan lynch mobs in Rock Springs and Thorndale. The paper attacked the timidity of the Mexican consuls who took no position on the lynchings and did not intervene in the cases on behalf of the Mexican nationals who had lost their lives.

In a one-year anniversary retrospective, editor Nicasio, Sr., and other writers of *La Crónica*, including Jovita, Eduardo, and Clemente Nicasio, look back at stories of the past and reaffirm a pledge to "defend with enthusiasm and frankness the interests of the Mexican Texans." The writers also reflect on attacks that have come their way from the paper's detractors and on the excellent contributing articles of the "liberal columnists of Texas and Mexico."

Nicasio and his family and the *Crónica* called for the *Gran Concilio de la Orden de Caballeros de Honor* to discuss the issues of the day—the loss of language and culture, civil rights, lynchings of Mexicans, education, and economic and labor conditions.

In 1911, the Idars hosted *El Primer Congreso Mexicanista*, a week-long political conference convened in Laredo to voice social grievances resulting from the Anglo-American domination of Texas-Mexicans. According to José E. Limón, professor of anthropology and folklore at the University of Texas at Austin, the Congreso was the culmination of the Idars' initiation "of a campaign of journalistic resistance" to several serious social and economic issues of the day, including the transfer of almost all Texas-Mexican land into

❖

Journalist Jovita Idar, considered fearless, outspoken, and forward thinking, did much to further the cause of civil rights of Mexican-Americans and women. She is pictured at the presses of the Spanish language news journal El Progreso, *the newspaper she published.*

A. I. IDAR AND ANITA PEREZ, SAN ANTONIO AND INSTITUTE OF TEXAN CULTURES

Anglo-Texan hands, an intensifying Mexican immigration, the conversion of the Texas-Mexican population into a cheap labor pool for the development of Anglo-Texan ranching and farming interests, the political and economic control of the Anglo-Texans over Mexicans, and the Anglo's deeply embedded sense of racial superiority that had created a pattern of local, officially sanctioned segregation between the Texas-Mexicans and the Anglo-Texans.

The outspoken and liberal weekly clearly enjoyed the support of local businesses. Front page advertisers included August C. Richter's El Precio Fijo Department Store and the Juan Treviño Mercantile across from Market Square, now the Laredo Center for the Arts complex. In one issue, the death of Senator E. A. Atlee is front page news, a story noting that Laredo Mayor Dario Sanchez has ordered flags flown at half-mast and that Mr. Atlee was a "liberal, tolerant man," a "*caballero* of good temperament and a model of courtesy and goodwill."

In another issue, the writers of *La Crónica* defend an editorial recently run called "*Tontos y Cobardes*" (Morons and Cowards). The death of 15 year-old Alfonso Grado is headlined "*Un angel más*" (One more angel.) The paper documents in travel notes that business owner Sr. Manuel Vizcaya Sierra has returned from San Luís Potosi and that Mrs. H.J. Hamilton and F.G. Benavides have returned from a trip to San Antonio. The issue of January 15, 1910 mentions that Mr. H. Borchers is looking for a cook for his home. There is news, too, of a piano concert at a clothing store called *El Palacio de Hierro* and news that Srs. Don Clemente Gutiérrez and Everardo Torres, owner and director, respectively, of a publication called *El Aldeano* in Uribeño, were fined 200 *pesos* and a year in prison.

La Crónica expands at length on the activities of the upcoming George Washington Celebration, including band performances, bullfights, horse races, the presentation of the key to the city to Pocahontas, a parade, *jamaicas*, *serenatas*, the carnival, bicycle races, and "cockfights and games not prohibited by law." Other news stories discuss a Mexican conductors' strike that is in the making in Mexico, bad and dangerous conduct—menacing behavior and shots fired—at upriver Minera, a mining settlement. Editorials discuss "*La Iglesia Católica y La Mujer*" (The Catholic Church and Women) and "*Mèxico Bárbaro*" (Barbarous Mexico).

Other advertisers included E. Salinas and Bros. Department Store, La Perla clothing store, and El Puerto de Mazatlán Panadería offering "*Pan Caliente*" (Hot Bread) north of the Plaza. Abraham F. Peña advertises that he operates a farrier and buggyworks business at 906 Hidalgo, while A. Bertani and La Casa de Armengol advertise the arrival of cane seed. F.H. Lithgow advertises City Drug, and Peter Leyendecker, P.P. Leyendecker, and G.H. Winch advertise their lumberyard at Washington and Santa María.

Eduardo Idar covered the news of the Lower Río Grande Valley while Jovita and Clemente Nicaso filed staff reports in Laredo. *La Crónica*'s liberal format and broad scope allowed ample coverage of cultural and arts events and included in its varied mix the publication of poetry and other literary pieces. Guest writers and columnists from across the state and Mexico were contributors to the pages of *La Crónica*.

Idar, Sr., a native of Port Isabel, moved to Laredo in 1880. He was an assistant City Marshall and a Justice of the Peace in Laredo. In addition to being a commercial printer and the publisher of a Masonic review called *La Revista*, Idar was a member of the Sociedad Mutualista Benito Juarez, vice-president of the Mexican and Texas Mexican fraternal lodge system known as La Orden Caballeros de Honor, and a labor activist in *La Alianza Suprema de Ferrocarrileros Mexicanos*.

Jovita Idar became the first president of *La Liga Femenil Mexicanista* (League of Mexican Women) which formed as a result of *El Primer Congreso Mexicanista*. *La Liga*'s first work provided free instruction for poor Mexican-American children. *La Liga* called for education of women on par with the education of men, holding to the credo, "Educate a woman and you educate a family."

In 1913, when the Mexican Revolution reached the border, Idar relinquished the sword of her pen to assist her friend Leonor Villegas de Magnon in Nuevo Laredo to care for soldiers injured in battle. The two women, along with the other women they enlisted, saved many lives. They formed *La Cruz Blanca*, a medical relief organization. Magnon and Idar, accompanied by Idar's brother, traveled in northern Mexico as nurses to the revolutionary forces.

Jovita Idar joined the staff of the Spanish language newspaper *El Progreso* and made short work, via an editorial protesting U.S. troops on the border, of offending the United States Army and the Texas Rangers. When the Rangers showed up to close down *El Progreso*, Idar barred them from entering the building. When the Rangers eventually succeeded in shutting down the paper, Idar returned to *La Crónica*.

Among the journalists of note who have written in and about Laredo and the border region was Jovita Idar. She was the first president of the League of Mexican Women and held to the credo, "Educate woman and you educate a family." Jovita Idar's service to her community and convictions was broad—she and "La Rebelde" Leonor Villegas de Magnón formed La Cruz Blanca, a relief organization, during the Mexican Revolution.

WEBB COUNTY HERITAGE FOUNDATION

Jovita Idar married Bartolo Juárez in 1917. They lived in San Antonio where Jovita opened a free kindergarten for Mexican-American children. She worked for the Democratic Party and served as an intepreter for Spanish speaking patients at Robert B. Green County Hospital.

She became co-editor of a Methodist Spanish-language newspaper, *El Heraldo Cristiano*.

The Grande Dame of It All: Mabel Cogley Wall

The best remembered chronicler of Laredo society was its *grande dame*, Mabel Cogley Wall, society editor of *The Laredo Times* for over four decades. A native Laredoan born in 1887 at the Cogley family home at Houston St. and Main, Mabel was the daughter of Miles Thomas Cogley and Rose Hungerford Cogley.

Just as it was the train that brought Miles Cogley, the father of Rose Cogley to Laredo, it was the train that brought William Wallace Hungerford, a civil engineer for the Texas Mexican Railway, to Laredo. Rose Cogley's brother, Louis J. Hungerford, became President and Chairman of the Board of the Pullman Company of Chicago Illinois. Born in Cincinnati, Ohio, Cogley was the only one of his nine siblings not born in Ireland. His marriage to Rose Hungerford of the railroad-building Hungerfords brought Mabel and Daniel Hungerford Cogley into the world.

Miles T. Cogley served as president of both the Texas Mexican Railway and of the Milmo National Bank. A tragic firearm accident en route to a hunting camp on the Zapata Highway claimed the life of Mabel's brother, Daniel, when he was 10.

Mabel attended local schools until she left at the age of 12 for the French convent of the Mesdames of the Sacred Heart in Cincinnati. Upon her high school graduation, she returned to Laredo and married a young West Point graduate stationed at Ft. McIntosh, Lt. Steven Barlow. They had two children, Margaret and Rosita. After the Barlows divorced, Mabel later married Judge John Cowles Wall.

She first came to *The Laredo Times* as a proof reader and then moved to advertising sales. "My grandmother drove her around on her sales calls, because my mother didn't drive," recalled Margaret Barlow Tish, the wife of the late Allen K. Tish, former co-publisher of *The Laredo Times*. "She became society editor when she stepped in as a substitute for the society editor at that time. She held that position for over 40 years," Tish said.

Petite, vivacious, intelligent, kind, and high mannered, Mabel Cogley Wall is well remembered by those who worked with her at *The Times* and those who had a social occasion to share with her.

She was a charter member of the Society of Martha Washington and member of the Pan American Roundtable. She was a lifelong member of St. Peter's Church parish.

Laredo investor E.H. Corrigan remembers the attention Mabel Cogley Wall accorded every person who came into *The Times* with news of a wedding or a social event. "All brides were important people, all weddings important events. She made a point of being accessible to everybody as she sat at that typewriter and took their stories," he said, adding, "She was generous with her time to all who approached her desk."

"She grew up here and naturally knew the background of many of the families about whom she wrote. Her parents lived here and she had that additional source of background information," Corrigan recalled.

"When she began to work with William Prescott Allen, the *Times* publisher, it was a happy combination. She admired what he was doing for Laredo and he admired her capability and determination. She had drive and much energy. She loved being a Laredoan. She loved Laredoans and it showed in much of what she had to write," he said.

"All her co-workers adored her and admired her. She was focused on the newspaper and on the pleasant life she lived. She walked from her nearby home on Houston Street across St. Peter's Plaza and down Matamoros to the newspaper office. She was very trim, always wore high heels, and always had on a different pair of earrings," Corrigan said.

"She and her son-in-law had a very special relationship. Likewise, her relationship with William Prescott Allen was also a special one, one of friendship and genuine respect. He was glad she was at the paper," Corrigan recalled.

Mr. Allen made a special occasion out of the observance of the birthday of Mabel's mother, Rose Hungerford Cogley. It was celebrated at the newspaper offices on a Saturday night. "In the party, there were always politicians, bankers, and business owners—many with their wives. These were people who would like to appear in the newspaper. Mr. Allen would pass around coins so that guests could play the slot machines he had brought in for the party. An invitation to be a guest

Mabel Cogley Wall was a chronicler of Laredo social events for more than 40 years. An energetic, kind, and high-mannered woman, Mrs. Wall's contributions to The Laredo Times *were well received.*

Mabel Cogley Wall, far right, at the wedding of protege Cordelia Casso Flores to Ricardo Flores. Also pictured is Mabel's daughter, Margaret B. Tish.

COURTESY OF CORDELIA C. FLORES

at these yearly occasions was desirable and much sought after. They were an important event in Laredo at that time," he said.

Corrigan also recalled that the Casso sisters—Hortencia, Cordelia, and Mapy—all worked with Mrs. Wall after they attended Incarnate Word College.

"When one of us left to get married, another one of us came to work with Mrs. Wall," Cordelia Casso Flores began.

"*Era una dama, una perfecta dama.* (She was a real lady, a perfect lady) I was very fond of her, and I learned a great deal about journalism from her. She was organized about keeping dates and events and her notes about weddings, showers, club meetings, recipe stories, and special social events. When I see stories in the paper today that appear long after the fact, I remember how hard she worked to have stories ready ahead of time so that once the event transpired, the story was mostly ready except for a few details," Flores said, adding, "She would have the Colonial Ball story ready way in advance. She wanted her news fresh. She was very organized and very particular about names and spelling," she continued. "It was the policy of the newspaper to be as correct as possible and as timely as possible," she said.

"Mrs. Wall said you didn't have to go to the parties, that you could use the telephone. She said people loved to talk about their parties. Every young lady who got married or had a shower was welcome to place news of her marriage in the paper. Mrs. Wall was very inclusive," Flores said.

"I learned about discretion from her, how important it is what you write and when you write it. There were many stories that didn't get in the paper. Only the ones that fit her sense of propriety went in. She went by the book, the etiquette book, on social issues. She was very maternal with me, very kind, very protective," she continued.

"Mrs. Wall practiced the Golden Rule. She always took the high road, and so did the newspaper. You never saw any advertisements for anything risqué or immoral. The newspaper was very conscious of good relations with Mexico and made every effort to cover both sides of the border and to be a good neighbor," Flores said.

"I loved that she was always dressed for tea and wore the appropriate accompanying beautiful jewelry. She was a wonderful conversationalist, very witty," she said. "She was also the diplomat of the office, the mediator if someone needed her intercession with Mr. Tish," Flores said.

"Editors came and went, but Mrs. Wall was always there. When I worked there in 1967, there was a core of individuals who had been and continued to be the backbone of the newspaper. There was Tom Green, Jim Parish, Alicia Mendoza, Guy Skipper, Clara Moreno, Joe Barrera, Mr. Zardenetta, Mr. Watts in the press room. Those were great days," Flores remembered.

"She was a dear friend to many. The relationship she had with her housekeeper, Chelo, was a very special one. She considered her a very trusted and much loved companion, and it was clear to everyone that the current of the friendship ran both ways, that Chelo was a dear and esteemed friend," Flores recalled.

JIM PARISH: A MAN FOR WHOM RIVERS & LANGUAGE KNEW NO BORDERS

When Jim Parish first came to *The Laredo Times* in 1961, the publication's office and physical plant were at the corner of Juarez and Matamoros, next to the Bender Hotel, west of the post office and the federal building. These were the days of manual typewriters, stories pecked out on newsprint and typeset once more in hot lead, linotype, line of type. Proofs were read on long galley sheets.

These were the days in which the *Times* was under the stewardship of Allan K. Tish, a serious, red-haired, flush-faced man known affectionately in the press room as "*El Huachinango*," the red snapper. The *Times*' advertising staff included H. A. Dwyer, Guy Skipper, and Abe Palacios.

Tish's hand was on the editorial rudder, but he had a history of hiring good newsmen like Lloyd Hackler, Jim Johnston, and Larry Jackson to keep company with the *Times* lifers, pulse-of-the-city journalists like Jim Parish, Tom Green, and Juan Vasquez.

Tom Green wore a Fedora. Jim Parish wore a *guayabera*. Mabel Cogley Wall, the society editor and Mr. Tish's mother-in-law, wore pearls and took her news near the front door with brides and mothers of brides. Carmina Danini, who would, over the next decades, enjoy a career of excellence in journalism and many professional accolades, was one of the *Times*' proofreaders.

In more ways than one, *The Laredo Times* made journalists out of eager upstarts and dedicated employees with a nose for news. In more ways than one, the presses roared back then.

In those politically incorrect days, cigarette smoke hung thick in the air at *The Laredo Times*, and soda vending machines were scarce in the building, a reality that necessitated a trip next door to the Bender Hotel for a cold ten-cent Coke or a cup of coffee. Jim was kind and nurturing, a man who called attention to good work and had distinct views on bad work or bad behavior. He was ever ready with consoling words after a new reporter had been called into the publisher's office for a little attitude adjustment.

"You did good, Kiddo," he would say, allowing the implicit possibility that an upstart reporter might make the cut and be doing this wordsmithing as a grown-up, too.

Through all the evolutions a newspaper can experience, through the move from private ownership to corporate ownership, the revolutionary changes in computers and communication, the merging of two newspapers into one, the sale of the paper from one media group to another, changes in management models and communication theories, the constant at *The Laredo Times* for many decades was Jim Parish, among the most genial and dependable members of Laredo's news community.

Jim Parish's dedication in a lifetime of newswriting were much admired. His public generosity and his generosity of spirit were evident when he took the most humble of news events—the news in someone's life—and made it substantive and credible in print.

Many remember his work ethic. He will be remembered as a trooper, a prolific writer, a writer not only of competent adherence to grammar and spelling, but an honorable newsman who wrote the plain truth.

This native son of Eufala, Oklahoma was born on January 4, 1922. A student of Latin American history and government, Parish was a graduate of the University of Texas. After graduation, he worked in Ft. Worth for the late Jack Danciger, a Texan who promoted Pan Americanism between the United States and Latin American countries. Parish served in the U.S. Navy during World War II from 1942 to 1946. He taught in San Ygnacio and Zapata, and while in Zapata, he began to write for *The Times* a series of *Reporter's Notebook* accounts about the life and times of the people of the region.

When downtown was the heart of the business community, Jim, a longtime resident of the Hamilton Hotel, was highly visible covering the events that moved and formed our city and this shared border.

Jim Parish was a man of this world, a traveler, a man for whom rivers and language marked no boundaries, a selfless man of immense kindness.

❖

Jim Parish, once a school teacher in San Ygnacio and Zapata, offered readers in Laredo a lifetime of service as a writer for The Laredo Times. *Parish, a native of Eufala, Oklahoma, was known to many Laredoans not only as a journalist, but also as a selfless man of immense kindness.*

CARMINA DANINI, WITNESS TO HISTORY

"I always thought I would be in this business," said journalist Carmina Danini, a writer for the *San Antonio Express-News*. "I was a bookworm who loved history. As a reporter, you see history as it is happening, whether it is live at the roadside scene of an accident or a shooting or an interview with the president of Mexico. You are not watching history on TV, you are witness to it and you will write it and your story becomes a footnote to history," the native Laredoan said.

"The truth, the substance of your stories, can make people uncomfortable. It is something you finally learn to stop worrying about as a writer. If it's a problem to hold people accountable for their actions, then just sell ice cream. That makes everyone happy," Danini said. "When you write those discomfiting stories, you can't hide. You have to be accessible to hear from those who hated what you wrote and those who want to tell you how much they appreciate the story," she continued.

"In writing, inaccuracy is the worst sin," Danini said. "You won't be sued because the grammar is bad, though it is also terribly important because much credibility is lost when the writer can't spell or use correct syntax," she said.

"We all have a story," Danini said. "Most people have a history about them, either personally or

Carmina Danini began her career in journalism as a proofreader and moved through the ranks of the Hearst Corporation to become the first chief of the Mexico City Bureau for The San Antonio Express-News *in 1994. She is still with* The Express-News *in San Antonio.*

about the way they did their jobs. Journalists ferret out that history. It was increasingly difficult to continue to write in Laredo, my hometown, as I did in the seventies and eighties. People I went to high school with, if they were the subject of a story I wrote, would come up to me and say, 'Hey, you were really hard on me in the newspaper!' I would say, 'Wasn't that you on the police report? Weren't you indicted for allegedly killing someone?' It is inevitable in the news writing business that you will burn some bridges behind you."

Danini, a 1963 graduate of Martin High School, came into the news business as a proof reader at the *Laredo Times* from 1967 to 1969, "Before the moon landing," she clarified. She returned to the *Times* from 1972 to 1974 and then attended the Doscher School of Photography in Vermont in 1975 before returning to Laredo to write for *Saludos*, a magazine owned by Pat and Connie Miller. "I covered the Tecolotes," Danini said, despite the fact that I knew nothing about baseball. "During a game I asked veteran sportswriter Matias Arambula when the half-time was and he took me under his wing to give me a better understanding of baseball. In this business, you can learn as you go along," she said, adding, "That was before Elvis died."

Danini took a time-out from newspapering to be the telephone operator at the Hamilton Hotel. "It was a Lily Tomlin set-up, not at all modern. I enjoyed my time there," she recalled.

With the advent of the publication of *The Laredo News* in 1977, Laredo became a two-newspaper town. Danini characterized her years with *The News* as "extremely turbulent." She said her time at *The News* was filled with new experiences and news stories that turned Laredo politics on its ear—such as the May 1978 federal indictment of former Mayor J.C. Martin, Jr., for mail fraud; and the establishment of city manager form of government for the City. "There was a newspaper war going on. These were exciting times. Sometimes they were fun," she said.

After a brief tour of duty as city editor of *The News*, Danini returned to *The Laredo Times* as a reporter in 1981 and wrote for the publication until she went to the *San Antonio Express-News* in 1990. She found a three-month exchange with Monterrey's *El Norte* "an extremely satisfying experience, one that called up all my experiences as a journalist, as a bilingual person, and as a human being who had grown up on the border.

"Knowing more than one language is so important. It allows you to experience and write about the world in more than one way," she stressed.

Danini holds dear the distinction and the experience of being the first chief of the Mexico City bureau for the *Express-News*. She spent 1994 and 1995 in Mexico City, witness to the tumultuous and tragic events, including the assassination of PRI presidential candidate Donaldo Colosio, that placed Ernesto Zedillo in power. "Those were very important years for me as a journalist," she said.

Writing of Colosio's "first and last stop in Tijuana," Danini reported, "Two shots rang out as Colosio strolled through the neighborhood, two short and not very loud blasts that changed the PRI and the history of Mexico politics forever."

Danini, never one to spare words, characterized Zedillo as "gray and dry, with all the charisma of a fried egg." She described her post-assassination hikes across the *incertidumbre* (uncertainty) of Mexico's political map as "garden paths, land mines, and shifting sands, a landscape dotted with the unprecedented."

Danini chronicled how the 'little' matter of Chiapas and its rebellion mushroomed and was unleashed when it was revealed the government had used its own troops to squash the insurrection.

The story Danini remembers best is not the one she filed about the fall of *patronismo* in Laredo—events to which she refers as "Laredo's equivalent to Watergate"—or about the murder of Colosio. It is a police story. There was a call to the Laredo Police Department from a housewife on Hidalgo St. who reported that the neighbor's cat had entered the open window of her kitchen and taken a steak left out to thaw on a table. The officer answered the call and wrote his report. Danini read the report, filed her story, and the story ended up on the front page of *The Laredo Morning Times*. "The police officer was furious. He came to see me and said he was the laughing-stock of his department. He wanted to know why the story was written, and beyond that, why it had merited the front page. The story, as it seems often to be the case, had an effect I had not anticipated," Danini said.

Carmina Danini was born in Laredo September 1, 1945, the daughter of Geuril and Josefina Danini, the sister of Josie Subik and Eloína Fudge.

MANITAS, MANITOS

THE THREE R'S: READING, WRITING, & REVOLUTION

Although her colorful life and heroic deeds are largely unknown in this region, Leonor Villegas de Magnon is an example of the caliber of idealistic, committed, and dauntless individuals this community has produced. Born into a prominent Laredo family, she grew up to become a heroine of the Mexican Revolution.

Leonor was born to Joaquin and Valeriana Villegas on June 12, 1876 in Nuevo Laredo. The family moved to Laredo, setting up their export business in a beautiful building on Flores Avenue. Their home above the store was considered to be one of the most luxurious of the time. After boarding school in New York and two years in Spain, Leonor married Adolfo Magnon, an agent for the train and steamship lines in Mexico City. The couple lived there until 1910, during which time Leonor had three children.

While living in Mexico, Leonor became involved in the political struggles against Dictator Porfirio Diaz. She wrote articles critical of Diaz which appeared in *La Crónica*, a newspaper published by the Idar family in Laredo.

Soon Leonor's father's businesses in Mexico were closed down in retaliation for the activism of his daughter. Leonor moved back to Laredo, to a small house at 811 Flores Avenue. Her husband, himself involved in the revolution, could not leave Mexico City and so their lives took individual paths from then on. Leonor's house became a meeting place for exiles fleeing the revolution.

THE BEGINNINGS OF *LA CRUZ BLANCA*

When fighting broke out in Nuevo Laredo on the morning of March 17, 1913, gunshots and cannon fire were heard in the two Laredos. Leonor and her friend, journalist Jovita Idar, quickly mobilized a group of women to tend the wounded in Nuevo Laredo. Venturing into the fighting, the women pulled the wounded to safety. Five American doctors worked alongside the women: Drs. H. J. Hamilton, A. W Wilcox, John T. Halsell, E. H. Sauvignet, and W. W. MacGregor. This was the beginning of La Cruz Blanca.

Relief squads were organized on the American side to help with clothes, food, and medicine. Some of the Laredo contributors were: M. T. Cogley, Ignacio Benavides, A. M. Bruni, A. C. Richter, Pedro Treviño, Julian Treviño, E. Salinas and brothers, and Borchers Bakery.

While Leonor's efforts helped save many, the problem of Carrancista soldiers getting back to their units arose. Leonor devised various way to spirit them out underneath the noses of their captors. When this was discovered, La Cruz Blanca was no longer allowed into Mexico. During the ensuing

❖

Top, left: Among those young members of the 1912 kindergarten classes of Leonor Villegas de Magnon were Anita Ligarde, Carolina Arce, María Luisa Martinez, La Güera Guardiola, Rafael Martinez, Raul Guerra, Delia Treviño, Tino Pappas, Sarita Aguilar, Consuelo Alexander, Luis Ochoa, María Antonieta Gonzalez, Pilar Valera, Carlos Palacios, Olga Ornelas, Berta and Nela Salinas, Beatriz Salinas, Pablo Gonzalez, Gabo Ochoa, Domingo Gonzalez, Olga Benavides, María Luisa Treviño, Nena de la Garza, Juanito Alexander, Licha Ligarde, Polo Villegas, Nina Aguilar, and Nina Gonzalez.

LEONOR M. SMITH COLLECTION

Top, right: Anita Bruni Ligarde and Lolita De Llano were among the kindergarten students of Leonor Villegas de Magnon who were photographed by the renowned photographer José García.

WEBB COUNTY HERITAGE FOUNDATION

❖

Above: "La Rebelde," Leonor Villegas de Magnon, and Aracelito García posed for this Cruz Blanca photograph during the Mexican Revolution.

COURTESY OF LEONOR M. SMITH

Below: Leonor Villegas de Magnon is pictured with members of La Cruz Blanca at Monterrey, June 28, 1914, including (standing left to right) Jesús Pérez Fierro, Captain Rodolfo Villaba, María Morales, Col. Eugenia Canales, Don Faustino García, and Eduardo Idar. Seated are María Villarreal, Villegas de Magnon, Lilly Long, and her son Robert.

COURTESY OF LEONOR M. SMITH

months of lull in the action, Leonor established a kindergarten in a hall owned by her brother, the first kindergarten in Laredo.

On New Year's Day, 1914, the Carrancistas again attacked Nuevo Laredo in a terribly fierce battle which caused great alarm on the American side. The International Bridge was closed. Leonor and volunteer nurses María Villarreal, Bessie Moore, and Lily Long, went into action. That night, one hundred wounded soldiers, brought across the river in skiffs, filled the emergency hospital. When Laredoans heard of it, mattresses, bed linens, food, dressings, and medicine began to pour in from neighbors, friends, and sympathizers. Americans and Mexicans worked side by side taking care of the wounded.

Leonor's kindergarten was transformed into a makeshift hospital and her young pupils became involved in the revolution, too. As she described it, "Their work tables had been made into beds, their little chairs, into bed tables. Each child was introduced to the reality of the Revolution at the sight of wounded soldiers who resembled the toy soldiers they had used in counting games."

(Credits: Bessie Lindheim's La Rebelde; *literature of the Webb County Heritage Foundation.)*

La Docha

Long before the advent of Loop 20, María Rodriguez, eluding all modern encroachments, lived like a holdout frontier woman on a tiny parcel of land northeast of Del Mar subdivision. People called her La Docha. She was archaic and uneducated, a tender of goats, and a woman utterly wise to the cycles of life and death, weather, the seasons, rattlesnakes, coyotes, and human nature.

There was a tendency in do-good circles in Laredo to pity La Docha charitably for she was nearly 80 and lived alone in a tiny two-room shack that had no plumbing.

La Docha, however, felt she lived in bounty. She said she was rich on the inside, and frequently cited what made her so—her health, an expanding herd, a comfortable house, friends, cheese, and milk. She said she was blessed and gave thanks often to a framed Virgin Mary and a variety of plaster *santitos* (figurines of saints) that decorated her home.

A small, round woman who wore a bandanna and a broad-brimmed straw hat adorned with plastic flowers and leaves, La Docha was exuberant and upbeat about her circumstances. She was grateful for the days that allowed her to enjoy her productive life as caretaker of *sanchas*, *chivos*, and *cabritos* (goats). She walked her herd daily to adjoining tracts for grazing. In a pink housedress, sweater, thick socks, and slippers, La Docha ambled at daybreak alongside the paved road, calling to the herd which followed obediently behind her in single file. She returned for them at day's end and repeated the maneuver in reverse.

She spoke convivially with her goats, calling them "Sancha, Pingo, Payasa" and other endearments. Clearly the animals were not simply sources of revenue and food—they were her dear companions, friends on the hoof. La Docha's goats—all 70 of them—behaved like pets who responded to their individual names and to her commands, chastisements, and endearments.

"I am as old as the year," she said in 1978. "Which one are we in?"

Walking with a wooden staff and with her goats in tandem like a dappled ribbon of browns, grays, and blacks, La Docha, in a flowered housecoat, ornate gold earrings, and striped

Raggedy Ann socks, cut a vivid figure against an already dramatic orange and lavender horizon.

Her conversations with her animals, the sounds of their hooves, bells and bleats, embellished the enveloping beauty of the *monte* (brushland) at day's end. *Chicharras* paused, and time quite nearly stood still as though it stood sentry on the periphery of her simple life with her herd of well-behaved ruminants.

La Docha loved to tease and laugh, and she communicated love and affection unencumbered by the newness of friendship. She appreciated the slightest kindness, and she reciprocated with good words over a cup of coffee. She had an odd, high-pitched voice that cracked with amusement and emotion. She made few references to the past except to say that she had been born in Encinal and that she had a sister.

"People worry about me, and they've asked me to move into town. But I won't," she said obstinately on a walk through the defoliated barnyard and to her fenced garden of chiles, tomatoes, and zinnias. Her pens were weathered planks, plywood scraps, and discarded political campaign signs wired together. After watching a nanny birth two kids late one winter afternoon, she said with relief, "I will sleep well tonight. La Blanca always has a hard time."

Goats followed La Docha everywhere, sitting when she sat, stopping in the barnyard when she stopped—ever eager for a kind word or a stroke behind the ears.

In warm weather we visited outdoors in the shed attached to her house, a shed which housed one of her few concessions to modern life—a prized, reconditioned turquoise Frigidaire that locked with hasp and padlock screwed to its exterior. "Look how well it ices—top and bottom," she said proudly as she opened both doors.

La Docha's two other concessions to the twentieth century were the electric fan and an ancient Philco radio in her cluttered little house, which was a lavender painted board- and-batten structure on a thin concrete pad. A brick hearth dominated one wall of the kitchen, and her mantle was festooned with mementos and keepsakes from friends. A china cabinet was stuffed with papers and notebooks, a few dishes and an array of religious statues. She kept addresses in an old spiral notebook with a hand-sharpened pencil stub.

La Docha, as María Aguirre was affectionately known to many Laredoans who befriended her, tended goats on a little plot of land near what is now the Loop 20 area. Through the seventies and part of the eighties, she was often seen, her herd of goats in single file behind her, along the unpopulated end of Del Mar Boulevard.

MARÍA EUGENIA GUERRA

The clutter of her home was well-ordered, the bare concrete floors dustless and impeccably clean. The floral patterned oilcloth was cheery on the ancient dinette table with curved metal legs.

In winter she walked outside with a visitor and then came in from the cold to drink boiled coffee from white enamelware cups in a kitchen that smelled of the diesel fuel she had used to start the hearth fire. In minutes, the fire roared and filled the little room with the heat that only a mesquite fire can provide.

At Christmas, bouquets of gay flowers and poinsettias bloomed from her furniture, from statues and from cracks in the walls of her house. Pictures of her many friends were stuck to the glass of the china cabinet with yellowed Scotch tape.

Her friends included neighboring ranchers, people who worked nearby, or Laredoans who had come to know her and had began to care for her by making sure she had a way into town for groceries, a doctor's appointment, or to buy animal feed.

Her bedroom was orderly and tidy, large enough only for bed and a matching chiffonier with drawers. The small house with its scaled down features and low metal roof had a gnome-like quality, a quality heightened by La Docha's stature and her jolly, elfin teasing.

Though La Docha lived in another time, she found no cause to butt heads with the present. She did not resist change; she simply was unable to use it.

The Sharkey Sisters: Vera & Anita

The sisters Sharkey, Vera and Anita, were born in Laredo on February 6, 1895, and

❖

The Sharkey sisters, Anita and Vera, were students at the Surrat private school.

COURTESY OF E.H. CORRIGAN

January 18, 1898, respectively, to Ernest E. Sharkey and Viola Delia Burkett Sharkey.

The sisters became exemplary, civic-minded citizens who were known to many Laredo youngsters as Mrs. Enckhausen and Mrs. Corrigan, women who would shape lives in their respective roles as the director of the Girl Scouts program in Laredo and as a Blessed Sacrament catechism instructor.

VERA

Vera Enckhausen, or Bab, as she was known within her family, married F.H. Enckhausen who came to Laredo's Ft. McIntosh with the Wisconsin National Guard during the Pancho Villa incursions. Vera and F.H. had two sons, Frederick Harry and William (Bill) Ernest Enckhausen. After living in Panama, Sault Sainte Marie, Michigan, and Pontiac, Illinois, Vera and F.H. returned to Texas. Fred Enckhausen worked for Central Power and Light in nearby Mirando City. The family lived in Hebbronville and then in Laredo once again, residing on Market Street in a home adjoining the Sharkey property. The low gray stucco residence had green shutters, a black iron fence, shade trees that kept the house cool in the summer, an open verandah facing Market Street. Vera is remembered by her niece Margaret Poling for her trademark long gray hair worn in a bun, immaculate white gloves, and a dress-up hat for outings.

Vera Enckhausen was a teacher at Central School. She became the social director of the local USO in 1943. She was the first Executive Director of the Laredo Girl Scout Council in 1947, a position she held until her death in 1959. She is credited with many of the changes in the Laredo Scouting program that sparked civic involvement and gave the program permanence and sustainability.

The Girl Scout House, which is located behind the Market Street Tennis Courts complex, was dedicated to her memory March 17, 1973.

Blue-eyed and white-haired like her sister Anita Corrigan, Mrs. Enckhausen is well remembered by Laredo Girl Scouts who had occasion to attend camp with her in Uvalde or any of the number of Girl Scout activities in and away from Laredo.

ANITA

When Anita Sharkey was born in 1898, Laredo was a city of 13,000, a city that enjoyed the conveniences of electric railway transportation, city lights, and a public waterworks system, as well as the economic benefits of the railway systems of two countries. The intersection of the international rail traffic of the Texas Mexican Railway and the Ferrocarriles Nacional de Mexico, S.A., figured largely in the life of Anita Sharkey, her marriage to Ed Corrigan in 1924, and the lives of their children Bartholomew, E.H., and Mary Alyce. Anita's father, Ernest Sharkey, worked for the Tex Mex Railway as a conductor. Her future father-in-law Bat Corrigan (Bat I) worked for the Nacional.

Like her sister Vera, Anita attended Mrs. Surrat's private school which was near the Sharkey residence and later *La Escuela Amarilla*, Central Elementary School. She was driven to school by horse and buggy and later took the streetcar to classes at old Laredo High which is now the home of La Posada Hotel Suites.

"They were similar but also dissimilar," recalled E.H. Corrigan of his mother and Aunt Bab, "Both very feminine, but distinctly different in build and demeanor."

Anita Sharkey Corrigan left behind a large body of *recuerdos* (mementos) in priceless scrapbooks that nicely piece together the Laredo in which she studied, grew up, and lived until her death in 1991. Those personal archives provide a valuable narrative for many of the social customs surrounding cultural events in Laredo throughout her lifetime.

Anita Sharkey was a member of the Sixteens, the 16 members of the Laredo High School graduating class of 1916 who held as their motto *In Omnia Paratus*, Ready for All Things. It was this class that named the first ever yearbook, *La Pithaya*. Newsclippings and dance cards in Anita Corrigan's scrapbook apprise of a Christmas "Girls and Boys Dansant" at the Latin American Club. An invitation in the collection informs that on December 28, 1915, Harry and Will Sames hosted a Christmas Party at the Elks Hall. Anita's dance card is filled with the names of the hosts as well as the names Ed Brewster, Randall Nye, Alden Muller, and Aaron Moser.

The scrapbook also chronicles many of the events surrounding the Washington's Birthday Celebration. Anita Sharkey was one of nine "peaches" who graced the Laredo High School float in the annual celebration. Others on the float were Irene Moser, Rowena Loftus, Alice Adami, Kate Brennan, America Meriwether, Gladys O'Brien, Mary Hall, and Elizabeth Bunn.

Graduation festivities for the Sixteen's included a dinner at the Bender Hotel, which was hosted by Anita Sharkey, Irene Moser, Vesta Sutton, and Eugenia Lafon; a hayride to Manadas Creek; a campfire breakfast hosted by the Junior Class at Manadas Creek; and the elaborate Shakespeare Tercentenary May Fête held at what is now known as St. Peter's Plaza. Graduation night was staged at the Royal Opera House. A local newspaper noted the Royal's balconies and aisles were "taxed to their utmost capacity." The graduation program was divided in half—the first a playlet staged by the 11 women and the five men graduates, and the second, the graduation exercises. The evening's entertainment opened with a rendition of the overture from Rossini's *Barbiere de Seville*.

Anita met Ed Corrigan at the Bella Vista swimming pool. They were married at St. Peter's Church by Rev. Father John Dubourgel. After a wedding trip to San Antonio, Corpus Christi, and Kerrville, the couple set up their household on Market Street. Ed Corrigan was a partner in the U.S. Customs house brokerage firm of Brennan and Corrigan. Anita and Ed had three children. Bat III, named after his grandfather and uncle Bartholomew, was born March 1, 1925. Edward Hal, E. H., was born March 5, 1927. Mary Alyce was born November 3, 1930. The family lived at 1312 Corpus Christi in a home built for them.

Anita's father Ernest Sharkey was one of 15 railroad employees and immigration and customs officials swept to their death in 1932 when the International Railroad Bridge gave way to the raging flood waters of the Río Grande.

Anita Corrigan's profile in social circles as a charter member of the Society of Martha Washington and a member of the Tuesday Music and Literature Club and the Pan American Round Table, was equaled by her role in civic and community activities and her devotion to the Catholic Church. She was a member of the Blessed Sacrament Altar Society, the Laredo Deanery of the National Council of Catholic Women, the Mercy Hospital Auxiliary, and the Webb County Tuberculosis Association. She was instrumental in the establishment of Blessed Sacrament Parish and the construction of the church building in the Heights. She is remembered by many of the children of Blessed Sacrament Parish as a devoted catechism instructor.

She was preceded in death by her husband who died June 10, 1956, and by her son Bat III of Brownsville, who died February 22, 1983. She is survived by her son, Laredo investor E.H. Corrigan, and her daughter Mary Alyce Corrigan, who with Jenny Leyendecker Reed and Betty Casey of MemoryBook Writers, gathered up and published *Cheers!* an amazing collection of anecdotal family history woven along real-time events.

Anita Sharkey Corrigan counted among her friends Mcafee Cullinan, María Treviño Leyendecker, Mabel Cogley Wall, Angela Borchers, Margaret Sames, Sissy Moser Shapu, Kika Yates Johnson, Chabela L. Gault, and Dr. Raúl de la Garza.

Anita and Vera Sharkey who became Mrs. Corrigan and Mrs. Enckhausen, respectively, shaped the lives of many Laredo youngsters, Mrs. Corrigan as a tutor and catechism teacher and Mrs. Enckhausesn as the Executive Director of the Laredo Girl Scout Council.

COURTESY OF E.H. CORRIGAN

MAX MANDEL: A CAREER IN BANKING BUILT ON FORWARD THINKING AND COMPASSION

"This is not the life I would have imagined growing up in Seguin. I thought I would have lived in Austin or San Antonio," said Laredo National Bank chairman emeritus Max Mandel of what he thought would follow his youth in Seguin or his graduation from the University of Texas School of Law. "I'm very happy that my life was here, that in 1938 I got a call from the law firm of Edward and G. Cullee Mann to come to Laredo," said the first generation American son of Hungarian Jewish immigrants who settled first in Floresville and then in Seguin.

The rest is history, and because Max Mandel has been so vital a component of the growth of Laredo, Mandel's history is also part of the history of this city and the history of banking.

"My life changed and moved into a new direction when I left Seguin for Austin, and especially when I came to Laredo. All that was Germanic, all that was sheltered, changed. Sometimes I think I became more of a Texan when I went to law school," Mandel said of the years he spent in Austin. He worked for the Mann law firm in Laredo until he began service in the U.S. Navy in 1941. "Mrs. Cullee Mann was persistent about wanting me to meet Roslyn Alexander. I was not as quick as Mrs. Mann would have liked me to have been, but I did finally meet Roslyn and we were married in 1942. It has been my good fortune that Mrs. Mann was persistent," he continued.

Lt. Mandel returned to the Mann firm after the end of World War II and worked there until he was offered a job as vice-president of the Laredo National Bank in 1950.

"Banking was new to me, but it didn't take long for me to realize that I liked it. I started off in the loan area and this is where I met people I would know the rest of my life—merchants and the employees of those merchants, ranchers, hard-working people. Laredo was a small town then. I liked having the opportunity one-on-one to talk to these customers of the bank. It gave me a great deal of pleasure to believe in what they wanted to do, to help them, and to see them succeed. Sometimes the loans were made on faith. You got collateral if you could, but sometimes you said yes even if you couldn't. We made loans for the college education of Laredo children and it is that which makes me feel that the career of banking was worthwhile, because I know that education can change a place," Mandel said.

"We made loans to people in the forwarding agency businesses and customs houses, some who, because they got help from us then, were able to grow as the city grew," he continued.

"Being part of this city's growth is one of the most rewarding things about being in banking," Mandel said, recalling that when he joined the bank in 1950, the bank had $20 million in assets. Upon retirement he had hoped to leave a bank with assets of $100 million. "It's now a billion-four," he said. "I think this bank has been part of many of the good things that have happened in this community, and I am proud of that role," he said.

"This was a small town when I got here. I think the population was at about 30 to 35,000 at the time. I always thought if we got to be a city of 100,000, that would be good. Even poised for NAFTA, I didn't think it would grow to this extent. Laredo was at the right place at the right time to benefit from the movement of increased freight between two countries. It's the luck of geography, a lot of opportunity, and how hard you are willing to work," Mandel continued.

"There was a core of us—other bankers, people in real estate, people in shipping, members of the Chamber of Commerce and the Laredo Development Foundation—who worked hard to push growth. We spent a good amount of time trying to foster the *maquila* industry in Nuevo Laredo and establishing solid relationships with companies in Monterrey. The sister cities of Laredo and Nuevo Laredo are naturals for dual plants and for shipping points. In Laredo we have places like Unitec and the Muller industrial area where everything is geared for the movement of freight. Laredo is on the main line, and this is where shippers want to be," Mandel said, adding modestly, "I think I played a role in that."

He believes new business should be courted more aggressively. "We have slipped a little. Companies and *maquilas* are still here and doing well, but there aren't any new ones coming in. We are not keeping up like I think we once did. McAllen as an example—they have industrial foundations that are very aggressive, very successful in attracting new companies to their area," he said.

"In Laredo there are some very smart, very innovative individuals in the business of warehousing and moving freight. You hear of their successes trying some new facet of warehousing. This is still a very exciting industry that relies not only on trucks but also on railroads," he said, "and on the ability of business owners to change and adapt to shifts in trade."

Seguin native Lt. Max Mandel and Roslyn who were married in 1942.

COURTESY OF MAX MANDEL

"I have learned through the years that *peso* devaluations are not the end of the world. There are very serious repercussions, but Mexico is a great country, a very resilient country. We all adjust," Mandel continued.

He lamented the loss of downtown as the hub of the central business district. "I'm very happy, however, that we have this beautiful old building," he said of the Plaza Hotel building which the bank occupies on the half block bounded by San Bernardo Avenue and Hidalgo and Farragut streets.

Mandel retired from banking in 1991. "I'm still a director, but I am not in the thick of things because banking has changed so much. I left banking just as it was becoming more complicated and very technical, and I think I was spared that. I think this business meant the most to me when I was in touch with how much you were helping people's lives change and grow. There weren't too many septuagenarians in my field when I retired," Mandel said. "I enjoy coming to my office every day to read *The Wall Street Journal*, *The San Antonio Express*, *Forbes*, the local papers, and business publications. I spend some time on family real estate ventures, things less demanding than being a banker," he explained.

"I think my most valuable work as a banker was to lend money to those who wanted an education or to the parents who wanted to send their children away for an education. Our children used to leave Laredo after they were educated. More and more of them stay here now to make this their home and to be part of the changes and growth. Nothing can create more change in a community than education. I am proud of the role of the bank in that change," he said.

"This town has a spirit, which at times I have perceived as lethargic and other times as dynamic. That spirit brought us back from the great flood of the fifties, and it has brought us back from *peso* devaluation after *peso* devaluation. We have always come back," Mandel said.

Though Max Mandel's dignity, kindness, and goodwill come from reserves deep within himself, he wears them on the outside. He will mention with unabashed affection the names of his wife and his children and grandchildren—three daughters, five grandsons, two granddaughters. He will talk about his years in banking and the growth of a city that he has adopted as his own and that has claimed him, but what he will never talk about—and need not mention, for these qualities are so well visible in his language and demeanor—are his business acumen, his forward thinking, and his compassion—the three things about him that have over six decades made Laredo move and change and grow.

"He's heads and shoulders intellectually above me," said attorney George Person, who has known Mandel for 30 years, "but he always makes you feel like you're his equal. He puts everyone at ease without compromising his position or condescending to anyone. He gets things done. He's never at a loss for what his objective is. He is a fine human being whom I have admired. I feel a deep love for him and the absolute highest regard for him. In business and in friendship, he has been a constant," Person said.

Johnson & Gill: Private Sector Public Servants

As you read through the history of the S.N. Johnson family in Laredo from the turn of the last century forward, the lives of Betsy Johnson Gill and Sam N. Johnson III come sharply into focus

Sam Johnson and his sister Elizabeth (Betsy) Johnson Gill and Lamar Gill.

COURTESY OF BETSY GILL

as vital members of the community who have taken seriously the early examples of community service set in place by their grandfather, Silas N. Johnson, and their father, Sam Johnson, Jr.

Native New Yorker S.N. Johnson, an astute businessman who came to Laredo in the 1880s, was the founder of the S.N. Johnson Bottling Works and the Coca-Cola bottling company.

His son, Sam Johnson, Jr., an attorney who joined the family bottling company and beer distributorship in 1930, served as the county attorney for Webb County and was also a county commissioner from 1942 to 1960.

Both men, in addition to fostering the prosperity and growth of the family's enterprises, offered exemplary leadership roles in the social, civic, and historical preservation events of the community.

"I respected and admired my father and the good example he was as a businessman, as a community leader, and as a preservationist," Betsy said. "It is a necessity to preserve our past, not just the buildings, but the memories of it, the oral history and the photographs. My father taught us that we learn from history," she said.

Betsy was born in Washington, D.C., Sam Johnson III, in Laredo. Though they lived some of their young lives away from Laredo with their mother, Elizabeth Kumpe, and their step-father, Edward F. Kumpe, an officer with the U.S. Army Corps of Engineers, they returned to spend summers with their father and grandparents. Betsy graduated from Our Lady of the Lake High School in San Antonio and Sam from St. Edward's High School in Austin. Betsy continued her studies at Incarnate Word College, and Sam served in the Army Air Force after high school graduation. After that stint in the service, he resumed his college education at St. Edward's University, completing a degree in 1951 and returning to Laredo.

Though Betsy and Sam followed different trajectories over the next two decades, Laredo continued to be the common ground that would shape their lives. "Laredo was our other home," said Betsy, "the place we came back to."

Upon the death of their father in 1961, both Sam and Betsy took leadership roles in the direction of the family business, Sam as president and sole owner of the S.N. Johnson Distributor and secretary-treasurer of the Laredo Coca-Cola Bottling Company, and Besty as vice-president of Laredo Coca-Cola Bottling Company from 1964 to 1987 and then as president from 1988 to 1992.

Betsy worked alongside her husband, L. Lamar Gill and her eldest son, Paul B. Payne, Jr., until their deaths—Lamar's in 1988 and Paul's in 1991.

It was after the sale of both the S.N. Johnson Distributor in 1990 and the Laredo Coca-Cola Bottling Company in 1992 that Betsy and Sammy turned their energies—lots of them—to support the arts, history, and culture of this region.

Betsy is a veritable whirlwind of community spirit in motion, a dynamo that moves from one meeting to another. An astute businesswoman and a fastidious record-keeper and archivist, she is a member of the Webb County Historical Commission, the Webb County Heritage Foundation, the Webb County Archaeological Society, the Laredo Center for the Arts, the Laredo Art League, Los Caminos Del Río, the City's Historic District Landmark Board, and the City's Tree Board. She has served on the Mayor's Blue Ribbon Ad Hoc Committee for the design of the new Laredo Public Library and on the Texas A&M International University Fine Arts Building Advisory Board Committee. She is an advisor to the Webb County 21st Century Committee. She is a proponent of higher education and has at times been the outspoken conscience of public servants, letting them know with immediacy when she has felt they have not served the public good.

Betsy Gill is a behind-the-scenes supporter of countless good deeds, some public and most private. She is the recipient of a special 1997 proclamation from the Webb County Commissioners Court that made May 27, 1997

"Elizabeth Johnson Gill Day" in Webb County. She is the mother of David Payne and the grandmother of Joanna Payne and Andrew Payne of San Antonio.

According to Sam Johnson, volunteerism came naturally to his parents. "They were both very involved in their community. During World War II, my mother was an organizer in Civil Defense in Portland, Oregon. She was the second highest-ranking person in the organization. She was thinking beyond her ken. She helped other people. We learned from both of our parents, as though it was a reflex to reach out to help those who needed it," he said, adding, "And always we learned to be part of the community we lived in, by learning about the community itself, its history and what cultural resources it had to offer. That was the case in Washington, DC, Portland, and Denver."

Sam spent summers working at the Coca-Cola plant. "As I got older, I took on jobs with more responsibility. I especially enjoyed being dispatcher or making sales at the dock. As I got older, I liked meeting a lot of people and being in a position to know what was going on in town and to work for things like Community Chest and the Chamber of Commerce," Johnson said.

A tireless supporter of the Laredo Little Theatre, Johnson has been active in local productions as actor, director, and stage hand since 1959. The LLT annually makes awards for outstanding work in his name, the "Sammies."

"For as long as I can remember, when we traveled with my parents, we stopped at museums and historical places. We were repeat visitors at Williamsburg and Mt. Vernon. Our maternal grandfather, Charles A. Korbly was a Congressman from Indiana, a Democrat. For as long as I remember, we had examples before us of role models of public service," Sam said.

He shares Laredo's history with visitors to the area who sign up for the trolley tours through the city's historical districts. "I enjoy the tours. Lots of people think I'm a teacher, but I'm really an actor. Teachers are on-stage the whole time they are in the classroom. I can't retain numbers or names well, but history sticks with me, and this city is rich with it," he said.

Sam is a parishioner of Blessed Sacrament Church. He is a member of the Caballeros of the Republic of the Río Grande, Laredo Little Theatre, Laredo Philharmonic Chorale, Laredo Philharmonic Orchestra, the Sons and Daughters of Liberty, the Washington's Birthday Celebration Association (WBCA), the Webb County Heritage Foundation, and the Webb County Archaeological Society. Sam portrayed George Washington in the 1979 WBCA events.

Margaret Sackville Jones: A Rare Hot House Flower

Margaret Sackville Jones was a self-taught botanist dedicated to the propagation and nurturing of cacti and succulents at the Cactus Gardens on San Bernardo Avenue. Though that quarter block of botanical wonder attached to the restaurant of the same name is long gone, the memory of Margaret Jones persists as a rare hot house flower whose plants were the passion of her life's work.

She came to Laredo from Canada by way of Dilley in the twenties. She was a botanical collector who scoured the mesas around Laredo for the unusual cacti specimens she propagated. As an aside to digging for cacti, she found and catalogued an extensive collection of Abasolo, Catan, and Tortuga points and flints. She was the official recorder of Laredo weather for the National Weather Service in the thirties and forties.

She was a tiny red-headed woman who went about her greenhouse work attired incongruously in dresses, tall shoes, hats, makeup, and costume jewelry. Her voice was high-pitched and she concealed a sharp sense of humor beneath a stern demeanor of correct diction and propriety.

She hardly let on if she liked you or not, though that message became clear in the gift of a cutting of something that bloomed an unusual color or the souvenir of a little clay pipe.

Given to sporting a khaki-colored pith helmet or a broad straw hat tied onto her head with a gossamer scarf, she wore cotton garden gloves as she went about her work. She spoke in halting Spanish to the men who worked in her greenhouse adjacent to the Cactus Gardens Cafe. She worked the cafe, but it was the gardens that held her interest. Her second husband, Augustus "Pappy" Jones, ran the cafe in the fifties and sixties.

The Cactus Gardens and Cafe were a museum of ancient and living things. Flints and points

The gardens were testimony to the will and drive of this independent woman who said she had borne in pre-war Laredo the then-scandalous stigma of divorce. The divorce, she said, had forced her to get on with her life and to do what pleased her.

Her command of Latin botanical nomenclature was phenomenal. She called her propagation stock by its true names—*Euphorbia cephalocereus*, *Kalanchoe beharensis*, and *Euphorbia jatropha*. Her collection was breath-taking and serious.

She was not fond of the common names such as Christmas cactus, bishop's cap, or old man cactus. Rather, she preferred the correct Latin *Zygocactus*, *Astrophytum*, and *Cephalocereus senilis*. She held a little disdain for the trendy appreciation of cacti as house plants for she had always loved them and did not like to think of them living in dark, damp places. She was a quiet, deliberate individual—reticent and stoic, though sometimes almost merry and affectionate with her plants, referring to mother plants and their pups. Her good friend Orvis Akers said she tucked them in at night.

❖

Above: The Cactus Gardens Cafe was a Laredo landmark on San Bernardo Avenue, as much for its outstanding array of cacti as for the pre-Colombian artifacts on display inside the restaurant.

Below: Roberto Peña with Margaret Sackville Jones, owner of the Cactus Gardens Cafe.

COURTESY OF ROBERTO PEÑA

and valuable pre-Colombian artifacts graced the cafe walls near the cash register. The restaurant with its rounded vinyl booths held the stale, cold atmosphere of air-conditioned smoke and fried food. Outstanding archaeological finds of ancient grinding stones, tools, and vessels marked the casual clutter on both sides of the steps and small porch of her house next to the cafe. The brick planters facing San Bernardo Avenue sprouted a forest of tall organ pipe cereus, which in winter Margaret Jones wrapped in newspaper to protect them from freezes.

The wood of the Cactus Gardens greenhouses was weathered and dry, like something living out its usefulness. The sandy loam in pots and beds was crusty, nearly lifeless, and the panes of glass had long ago taken on the opaqueness of decades of dust and water spots.

It was the wild, white roots in warm soil and the lustrous growing tips of plants in outrageous shades of green and gray-green that teemed with life. On damp, rainy days the still, thick atmosphere of the greenhouses quite nearly hissed with the industry of photosynthesis and regeneration.

Vast banks of spiny *Euphorbia grandicornis* and rust-tipped *K. beharensis* reached with ghost-like arms to the sun. Epiphytic cacti sprouted vibrant creamy blossoms emitting faint essences of intoxicating perfumes. "Don't sniff that one," she admonished near the incredibly showy maroon and white flower of a *Stapelia nobilis*. "It's pollinated by flies," she added, warning that, though lovely, the flower emitted a foul odor.

Margaret Jones was a dedicated collector, a seasoned, pith-helmeted observer and participant in evolution and life cycles.

❖

The Texas-Mexican Railway Depot at Benavides, Texas as seen in a photograph taken in May 1931.

COURTESY OF TEXAS MEXICAN RAILWAY

TRANSPORTATION

TEX MEX RAILWAY

An effort to bring rail service to Laredo, chartered at first in 1856 and then again in 1866 and once more in 1873 and finally in 1875, came to fruition at last under the leadership of banker, hide trader, and insurance agent Uriah Lott, the man who would begin to build the narrow gauge Corpus Christi and Río Grande Railroad.

Investors in the railroad included Richard King and Miflin Kenedy, Laredoans Meyer M. Levy, C.M. McDonnell, and Henry Goldschmidt, and the Philadelphia steel makers Andrew J. And James J. Dull. Construction of the undercapitalized railroad, which started off with only $39,000 in cash and $161,000 in promissory notes, moved only as quickly as Lott could collect from subscribers. The first spike was driven on November 26, 1876. In early 1877, 25 miles of track had been laid from Corpus Christi to Banquete. By 1879, the tracks had reached San Diego and Lott continued construction into the brush, stopping in hopes that Laredo would offer a bonus to bring the railroad to the city.

In 1881, Laredoans held three offers for railroad service. Besides Lott, offers came from Jay Gould's International & Great Northern (IGN) and Mexico's Ferrocarriles Nacionales de Mexico, which was managed by the Palmer-Sullivan Syndicate of Colorado Springs.

In need of a point of entry into Mexico that was not controlled by rival railroader Jay Gould, Gen. William Jackson Palmer offered to buy the yet-to-be-completed Corpus Christi and Río Grande Railroad from Kenedy and Lott who agreed to sell for a figure somewhere between $1 million and $5 million. The Texas Legislature granted a charter with the name of the Texas-Mexican Railway Company on June 30, 1881.

Even before a charter was secured, Col. W.W. Hungerford began grading roadway on both ends of the 102-mile stretch between San Diego and Laredo. On July 10, 1881 service was opened between Corpus Christi and Aguilares. While Laredo waited for completion of the remaining miles to the city from Aguilares, the company built a machine shop in the Heights, a warehouse, freight depot, and passenger depot. The City of Laredo built bridges across Zacate and Chacon creeks. A permanent railroad bridge was built across the Río Grande in 1883, replacing an earlier temporary bridge. On September 10, 1881, the rails crossed into the Laredo city limits.

Right: The familiar green and orange Texas-Mexican Railway engines have been part of the commerce of South Texas for over a decade.

COURTESY OF ARTURO DOMINGUEZ

Below: The Texas-Mexican train depot at Bruni.

COURTESY OF ARTURO DOMINGUEZ

The completion of the 162 miles from Corpus Christi to Laredo was celebrated with an inaugural excursion to Laredo, reportedly a raucous and spirited ride in the company of railroad tycoons, lawyers, scientists, bishops, and musicians.

In 1882, an additional five miles of track were constructed to the mining area above Laredo. Those tracks were abandoned in 1885.

A month after the Texas Mexican Railway Company arrived in Laredo, Gould's IGN arrived. Another of Uriah Lott's railroads, the San Antonio-Aransas Pass Railroad, crossed tracks with the Tex Mex at Alice. The St. Louis, Brownsville, and Mexico, later the Missouri-Pacific, reached the Tex Mex at Robstown in 1904.

The Mexican National Railways built its machine shops in Laredo, employing 200 mechanics. By 1889, the railroad could run a train from Canada to Mexico City. Also in 1889, the offices of the Texas Mexican Railway were moved from Corpus Christi to Laredo.

In 1895, the Tex Mex's iron rails were replaced with steel and its tracks converted to standard gauge. The switch was made July 17, 1902. In 1906, the line switched from burning mesquite logs to coal, and in 1920 to oil burning engines.

The growth of the railroad and the cargo it carried mirrored the growth and history of South Texas and Laredo. Agricultural and ranching products—including wool, cattle, and produce—were the primary cargo carried by rail from the turn of the century until the 1940s. Hebbronville was one of the largest cattle loading centers in the country, shipping tallow, hides, beef, and cattle on the hoof. The Tex Mex was the principal shipper of Bermuda onions from the river bottom farms north and south of Laredo. The transportation of coal was one of the railroad's mainstay cargos from the early 1880s up to World War I.

Oil exploration in 1921 around Mirando City and Torrecillas (Oilton), and discoveries near Corpus Christi, added petroleum to the list of products the railroad carried.

With its profitability ensured by the steady growth of South Texas, the acquisition of Tex Mex was sought on more than one occasion by the Missouri Pacific.

Under the leadership of president R.W. Morrison, the railway made railroad history when it converted all its locomotives to diesel electric in 1939, setting the precedent for the rest of the industry. The Texas Mexican's traditional roundhouse was replaced by a modern machine shop geared to diesel engines.

Facing competition from highway transportation after World War II, the Texas Mexican Railway changed to meet new challenges. A drop in cattle shipments was replaced with shipments of cotton, grain, beans, auto engines, and goods used for manufacturing. In 1950, the Tex Mex manifests showed that the railroad had shipped $1.7 million in manufactured items; $367,000 for mining products; and $9,000 for cattle.

When the railway celebrated its 100th birthday in 1975, almost 90% of the Tex Mex's rails had been replaced or upgraded over the last 25 years. The Piggy Back System (trailers atop flat cars) came on line. The agricultural packing sheds of the early days of the railroad were replaced with the warehouses and offices of U.S. customs brokers. In 1980, the Tex Mex opened a 30-acre industrial part east of Laredo on Loop 20.

The Mexican government sold the Tex Mex

❖

Sames Motor Company which has operated in Laredo since 1910, had its beginnings as the Laredo Auto Sales Company, which was established by William J. Sames and James Moore. Ford vehicles were originally sent to Laredo unassembled.

COURTESY OF HANK SAMES III

line in November 1982 to Transportación Marítima Mexicana, which sold 49% of the railway to Kansas City Southern in 1995.

The major export to Mexico in the late 1970s was grain. Exports from Mexico were scrap metal, cotton clothing, baling twine, ore, zinc, lead, sheet metal, cement brick, basketry, coffee, tobacco, fruit and vegetables.

Referred to as Lott's folly in its early days, the Texas Mexican Railway has enjoyed 125 years of prosperity while providing vital transportation and shipping services to South Texas.

Withstanding Revolution, War, & *Peso* Devaluations, Sames Motor Company Moves Along the Century Mark

"We've grown with Laredo," said Hank Sames III of Sames Motor Company, the Ford dealership which was established in 1910 by his great-grandfather William J. Sames and partner James Moore. "The business really has grown as the town has grown."

"I feel real privileged and honored," Sames said of running the company his great-grandfather started. "It's a lot of responsibility to keep it going. They survived many downturns—World War I, World War II, *peso* devaluations, the Mexican Revolution, more *peso* devaluations, the boom and bust cycles of natural gas exploration..."— during which Sames says the business was at times shut down, except for the service department which remained operational. "They survived all that, so I feel like it's my

Proprietors William J. Sames and James Moore pictured in front of Sames, Moore, & Co., a wholesale grocer, real estate brokerage, and onion growing enterprise.

COURTESY OF HANK SAMES III

responsibility to keep it going and pass it on to another generation."

Sames represents the fourth generation of the family in the auto business. His great-grandfather William Sames was originally from Connecticut and had gone to Cuba to sell life insurance. When that venture proved unsuccessful, William worked in Yucatan with archaeologist Edward Thompson in the Chichen Itza dig. Later, while in Monterrey, William developed pneumonia, and was told to return to the United States for his health. He arrived in Laredo in the 1890s. He met his future wife Virginia Wright, who ran the boarding house where he stayed. William took a job with a wholesale grocery owned by J. O. Nicholson, and became friends with the man's nephew James Moore. The two young men eventually bought the grocery, and it became the original Sames Moore Company, a partnership that lasted until 1925 and dealt in a wholesale grocery business, brokerage, onion growing, and farm and city real estate.

In 1910 Sames and Moore opened the Laredo Auto Sales Company as another venture when Ford began offering auto franchises. The operation began with the purchase of three Ford automobiles, which were sent unassembled by train. "Basically, you got a freightful of cars and assembled them yourself," Hank Sames said. The original three cars were sold from a grain warehouse behind the Sames-Moore Wholesale establishment.

The business expanded over the years in Laredo as the auto industry exploded all across the country. Laredo Auto Sales moved to a new location downtown across from the Hamilton Hotel in 1914, and opened a second location and garage on Jarvis Plaza. A newer location in 1919 followed on Houston Street. The first cars in Duval, Dimmit, Jim Hogg, LaSalle, and Zapata Counties were sold from Laredo Auto Sales, with dealerships later expanding to Alice, Encinal, Hebbronville, and Mirando City. Sales grew from less than a dozen cars in 1910 to about five hundred in 1922 to more than one thousand in 1926.

Presently, Sames Motor Company has four dealerships in Laredo: Auto Plaza on San Dario in North Laredo, the Calton Rd. location established in 1985, the Loop 20 & Highway 83 location established in 1992, and the Sames Honda dealership, acquired in 1995 and relocated to the current Honda site in 1997. "That was really the first Honda store of that type in the country," Sames said. "It's the new prototype."

Sames noted that in 1998, Sames Motor Company sold 2,500 new cars and 1,500 used cars, the present level of a growth curve that has seen an annual 30 to 40 percent increase in the past four years. As for projected future growth, "Well, we want to sell more, obviously," said Sames.

Sames has contributed to the community that has supported the business through the establishment in 1997 of the Ford "Salute to Education" Scholarship Program in Laredo. Thirty $500 scholarships were presented to Laredo high school seniors the first year, 40 in 1998, and 50 will be awarded this year. "I'm proud to be here," Sames said.

Sames said his great-grandfather decided to stay in Laredo because William Sames saw great potential here. Hank Sames feels the same way. "Our goal is to grow as Laredo grows. It's not going to stop for a while."

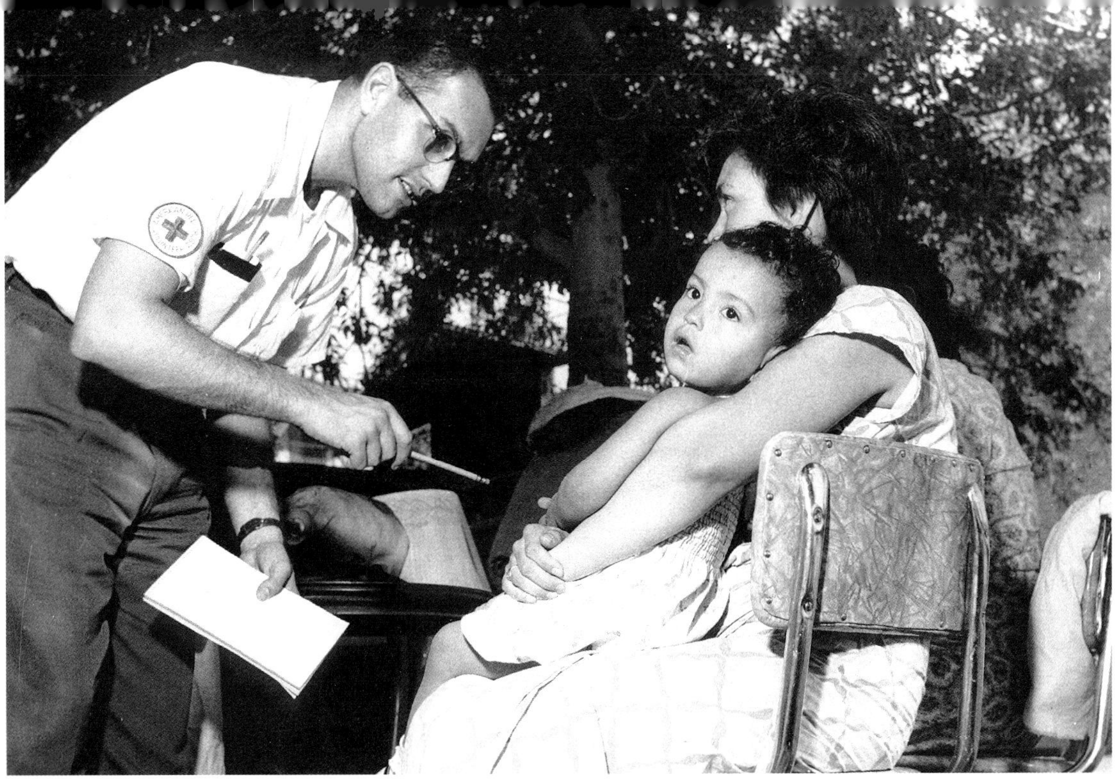

The Flood, 1954

The Río Grande left its banks on June 29, 1954, coursing fear that ran through the twin cities in a rush of roiling, brown water. The Flood of 1954 crested at 61.35 feet and flowed at 715,900 feet per second.

The river had become a wide, brown torrent, its velocity and breadth updated at regular intervals by radio broadcast. The jangle of the telephone brought the latest news. There were preparations—filling new galvanized garbage cans with clean water from a friend's well, putting aside emergency food and blankets. Even for those who lived far from the river, the idea of the flood was still troublesome for those whose family members worked through the night to help evacuate residents along the Zacate and Chacon creeks that were swelling with runoff. To a child, a flood sounded like it had a mind of its own, like it could sweep you away.

As the river widened, the tones of adult conversation became weighted with the seriousness of the impending rises and flooding that moved downriver to Laredo.

In the course of an afternoon, it became clear that parts of the city would be under water and isolated from other parts, and the ranch land surrounding Laredo would become inaccessible. Hard rains upriver at Piedras Negras and Eagle Pass had claimed drowning victims. Before the International Bridge washed out, before water started running over its top, before parts of the city became islands, the creeks around town filled quickly with backed up river water and spilled their banks. These were creeks that had hardly held more than a little rainwater. North and south, the river had become an endless fury of frothy swirling eddies, a river with a pulse of its own, a steady rush of force moving south. Occasionally, it was possible to make out some of the debris in the swirls—broken trees, sheet metal, and parts of houses and buildings. Manadas Creek began pouring into San Bernardo Avenue, cutting off the city to the north on Highway 81.

Newspaper accounts of the time document Laredo's response to the impending disaster from a river that would crest at 62 feet, leaving in its spent fury a wide swath of destruction that tore away the International Bridge and inundated much of Nuevo Laredo and low lying areas of Laredo along the creeks that fed into the Río Grande.

Initial reports of possible flooding seemed improbable, for the Río Grande had been so dry in 1953 that it had ceased to flow at Laredo. The small amounts of rainfall that had fallen that spring made flooding seem even less possible. It was the five-inch rains at Eagle Pass, however, that made the first

When the Río Grande left its banks in 1954, volunteers, the National Guard, the Red Cross, and the City's health department mobilized to provide typhoid inocculations and to provide clean water to Laredoans.

WEBB COUNTY HERITAGE FOUNDATION

❖

Above: This historical photograph shows that in May 1953 the Río Grande ceased to flow.

Below: A year later Laredoans and Nuevo Laredoans traversed the International Bridge on a pontoon bridge built by the Army Corps of Engineers after a June flood wiped out a good part of the steel and concrete bridge which was originally built in 1940 by a private developer.

WEBB COUNTY HERITAGE FOUNDATION

rise of 10 to 15 feet in the river. Hurricane Alice, which had touched land at Brownsville, brought two-inch rains inland to Laredo on June 25 and 11-inch rains upriver at Langtry and Bracketville on June 28. It was these rains that turned the Río Grande into a terrifying current of chocolate colored water thick with mud, debris, and the ruin of lives and homes. It was these torrents by which the Río Grande reclaimed the name found on old Spanish and Mexican maps—El Río Bravo del Norte.

Radio bulletins became more urgent as the river grew in width, depth, and velocity. The streets from the Heights neighborhood to downtown were closed off. Water covered the International Bridge and rose through downtown. The U.S. Customs lot washed away, and the flood began to lap at Convent Avenue, seeping into the stores closest to the river. In Nuevo Laredo, the entire familiar river bank was missing as water covered the first story of the Mexican *aduana* (customs house.)

From Price Street it was possible to see the shiny ribbon of Chacon Creek that had pooled inside the Big O Ranch and crossed the Freer Highway to back up nearly to the dam at Lake Casa Blanca.

There was a gravity to those days, a pervasive foreboding as Laredoans waited for the river's crest.

Response to the needs of both cities was nearly immediate. The National Guard brought amphibious vehicles to rescue stranded residents. Air Force helicopters plucked people from the river and from the tops of buildings. The Red Cross set up shelters across town. Newspapers were filled with awesome accounts and photos, and the radio station broadcast in subdued tones news of the damages to our town. Water and sewer lines were cut off in the city. Phone service to Nuevo Laredo was gone.

The City Health Department mobilized for typhoid inoculations and for clean water distribution. Laredo had become an island cut off from San Ygnacio, Zapata, Hebbronville, Freer, Houston, San Antonio, and Mexico, now accessible only by air or boat.

Typhoid serum was flown in immediately. Laredo doctors staged a series of three mass inoculations at Martin High and Central School.

Newspaper photos record the unordinary sight of evacuees and their furniture in the yard of Heights School. *The River of No Return* with Robert Mitchum and Marilyn Monroe was announced on the downtown theatre marquee. There was news, too, of the sad, eerie irony of a drowning death just after the waters subsided, even though there had been no loss of life to the actual floodwaters.

The waters had thundered south, spilling into the Falcon Reservoir, revealing that three 150-foot sections of the International Bridge had indeed been torn away by the mass of steel and concrete of the destroyed Laredo railroad bridge and the Piedras Negras bridge.

Parts of the city were coated in thick mud that was scraped with shovels and grader blades. Some of the mud washed away but much of it became a film of dust that lingered over the city that summer, an unpleasant reminder.

Life resumed as much normalcy as possible in those days after June 30. Most streets and cross-town bridges had opened by July first. People and their furniture left the shelters for their lowland homes to face devastating losses or lucky misses. Falcon Lake downriver filled with a million acre-feet of water, a volume that had not been anticipated for years to come.

Upriver it became a desperate reality that a dam on the Río Grande was needed at Del Río.

The waters subsided, and the creeks receded, leaving almost unbelievable high water marks of amassed brush and debris on the banks. The sister cities were cut off from each other and would be until the Army Corps of Engineers constructed a temporary pontoon bridge across the river. A single lane pontoon bridge accessible only by special permit was constructed immediately, followed by a wider double lane pontoon bridge with a sidewalk.

In the retrospect of memory and microfiche, it appears that the Flood of 1954 was a giant photo opportunity for the state, city, and county officials who took turns praising not only each other, but also themselves and their Mexican counterparts in Nuevo Laredo and Tamaulipas. On a daily basis, the newspapers just after the river crest were chock-full of photos of the mayors of both cities, together and posed individually with the governor of Tamaulipas; Texas Governor Allan Shivers; a National Guard colonel; the sheriff; a U.S. senator; Red Cross and Civil Defense personnel; in an airlift to Nuevo Laredo with Laredo Air Force Base pilots; with a colonel from the Army Corps of Engineers; and with Sen. Lyndon B. Johnson promising a push for the Amistad Dam Project at Del Río.

The *políticos* deserved recognition, for they had done their essential parts to secure federal grants to re-build the ruined water system and the parts of the city, to garner low interest loans for homeowners, and to find money for disaster funding and emergency staples.

The true life and limb heroes, however, were the Guardsmen in their amphibious "Duck," pilots and airmen from Laredo Air Force Base, city and county employees, firemen, policemen, and the countless citizen volunteers who evacuated Laredoans from their homes to higher ground.

Within ten days of the flood, after every last proclamatory photo opportunity had been exhausted, front page news in *The Times* resumed coverage of French incursions in Hanoi, Indochina; the ongoing saga of the Duke of Duval; the fall of President Jacobo Arbenz Guzman in Guatemala; the fall of Tegucigalpa to anti-Communist forces; and the revolting antics of Senator Joseph McCarthy.

Danger moved out of the city as quickly as it had come, leaving mud, debris, destruction, and the knowledge that our town had rallied to survive and minimize the ruthless, pounding course of a wayward river. The river's assault had made heroes of rich and poor alike, those who *mano-a-mano* had helped the other.

❖

Top, left: Guadalupe Street at Marcella and the cross-town rails during the 1954 flood.

WEBB COUNTY HERITAGE FOUNDATION

Top, right: Laredoans were well prepared for the Flood of August 1998. Nuevo Laredo and City of Laredo crews removed the rails of the Gateway to the Americas Bridge (Bridge I) to minimize damage should flood waters cover the bridge. The palm trees to the right of the bridge are in the parking area of Dos Laredos park which was severely damaged by the flood.

Below: Nuevo Laredo was hardest hit by flood of August 1998. In a scene reminiscent of the 1954 Flood, the Mexican Aduana facility took on serious flooding.

Laredo's Bridges

LAREDO WORLD TRADE BRIDGE IV

Lanes: 8.

977 feet in length.

March 15, 2000 Phase I.

September 15, 2000 Phase II.

Border Station includes: 8 Toll Lanes for Mexico Bound Traffic.

8 Primary Inspection Lanes for U.S. Bound Traffic.

A 100-bay cargo dock for complete cargo inspections.

Southbound truck queing for 310 spaces, expandable to 530 spaces.

Truck X-Ray Facility.

4-Lane Exit Control Facility.

Connecting roadways: Approach roaday to connect with Loop 20 (under construction), FM 1472 via approach roadway. Interstate 35 via Loop 20 interchange (under construction), and Mines Road (FM 1472).

GATEWAY TO THE AMERICAS BRIDGE

Local Names: Convent Street Bridge, Old Bridge, Laredo-Nuevo Laredo Bridge I, Puente Nuevo Laredo, Puente Viejo

4 Lanes; 1,050 feet in length

Originally constructed in 1940 and subsequently purchased by the City of Laredo from a private owner in 1946 for $695,000. Destroyed by flood in 1954 and re-built in 1956. Insurance paid the bulk of re-construction on the U.S. side of the bridge. The City of Laredo financed $300,000 in re-construction dollars through revenue bonds.

The bridge was built without a presidential permit, which was required only after 1972.

The General Services Administration owns the U.S. Border Station, which was constructed in 1940 and renovated in 1990.

Connecting roadways: On the U.S. side, near U.S. 83, I-35 and State Loop 20. Convent Avenue and Matamoros/Guadalupe Street run on with U.S. 81 and Matamoros Street, which connects with U.S. 83 and State Loop 20. In Mexico, near MEX 2, MEX 85, or MEX 1.

LAREDO-COLOMBIA SOLIDARITY BRIDGE

Local Names: Colombia Bridge, Puente Solidaridad, Puente Colombia, Puente Internacional Solidaridad Colombia, Bridge to Nowhere.

8 Lanes.

1,216 feet in length.

Owners: City of Laredo and the Government of Mexico. The State of Nuevo Leon has the concession until 2007.

The Colombia Solidarity Bridge was completed July 31, 1991 and financed by an estimated $12 million in revenue bonds in 1990.

The City of Laredo and Webb County were issued a Presidential Permit on May 8, 1990.

The General Services Administration owns the U.S. Border Station which was constructed in 1991.

Connecting roadways: On the U.S. side, FM 255 and FM 1472 (Mines Road). On the Mexican side, MEX 2 (La Ribereña).

JUAREZ-LINCOLN BRIDGE

Local Names: Bridge #2, Puente Juárez-Lincoln, Laredo II

6 Lanes; 990 feet in length.

Opened November 26, 1976.

The Juarez-Lincoln Bridge construction was financed by the City of Laredo throiugh an estimated $8 million in revenue bonds.

The General Services Administration owns the U.S. Border Station which was completed in 1982. The import lot was modernized in 1993.

Connecting roadways: On the U.S. side, near U.S. 81, I-35, and State Loop 20. Matamoros/Guadalupe Street connects with U.S. 81, I-35, and Loop 20. In Mexico, MEX 2, near MEX 85, and MEX 1.

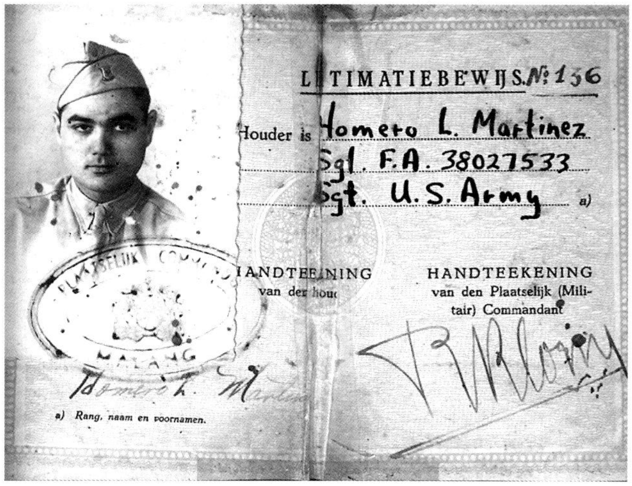

❖

Above, left: Sgt. Homero Martinez of the U.S Army's Second Batallion, 131st Field Artillery.

Above, right: The emblem of the U.S. Army Cavalry.

COURTESY OF ALICIA MARTINEZ

War

The Battle Became not the War, but the Battle to Stay Alive

"There is nothing heroic about wanting to stay alive," said former Prisoner of War Homero Martinez. "Nobody dies willingly except for the very old and the very ill," he said modestly, referring to his war experiences as "a period of impressive incidents."

Martinez was captured by the Japanese on June 8, 1942 and was freed August 6, 1945, enduring and surviving unimaginable deprivations and cruelty at the hands of his Japanese captors.

"What I thought war would be was far from what the experience was," Martinez said, beginning his story of war at the beginning.

Following the lead of his enlisted friends Jimmy Marinos, Albert Ochoa, and Nesto Samuels, Martinez enlisted in early 1941. "Telesforo Gutierrez and I went to the local board and enlisted," Martinez recalled. "We went to a local doctor for our physical. Foro passed and I flunked because I wore glasses. I argued with the doctor, telling him I'd already given my employer notice and that they'd already given me a farewell party, and I had told my girlfriend I would be back in a year," he said. "The doctor said, 'I can see that this could be very embarrassing.' The next time I had my eyes checked for a physical, I was wearing my glasses," Martinez said.

"We left for San Antonio by train on February 21 at 9 p.m. It was the second time in my life I had been on a train. We arrived at 2 a.m. and were given our mattresses and pillow and were sworn in the next morning. We were in San Antonio for six weeks. We were sworn in once again at Ft. Bliss, to which we traveled by troop train—65 men per car, seven cars. I was assigned to the cavalry. I used to love horses until I went into the cavalry. We performed all duties having to do with horses and tack. We rode on McClellan saddles and we learned gaits—walk, trot, canter, and gallop. At that time Jeeps had yet to supplant the horse. Everything we did had to do with horses and their maintenance and the maintenance of saddles, our boots and uniforms. I was at Ft. Bliss two months. I asked for a transfer to the motorized artillery. I made corporal in two months because of my secretarial and accounting skills," said Martinez who after high school had worked for the *South Texas Citizen* newspaper when it was owned by Manuel González and Frenchy Didieu, and then later as an accountant for Walsh Motor Co., the Hudson-Packard dealer in Laredo.

"Our regiment was split in two, and I ended up in the new one, a training battalion made mostly of hometown college boys and cowboys from Central Texas. I got into a fight when a sergeant called me a "taco vendor." I ended up in garbage patrol and gave up fighting. I had lost as many fights as I had won," he said.

Martinez' unit went to Camp Bowie in Brownwood, Texas and then to Shreveport and Lake Charles, Louisiana for field maneuvers. "I got to come home for two weeks before we were prepared for service in the Philippines. After our leave, we took the train from Camp Bowie to Fort Mason in San Francisco and then a ferry to Angel Island. From Fort Mason, we boarded an Army transport ship, the U.S.S. *Republic*, an ancient Merchant Marine passenger ship that the U.S. had gotten from Germany as part of World War I reparations. The *Republic* carried over 3,000 men, including our field artillery battalion, airmen, and a tank brigade from Wisconsin. Our battalion had become a detached battalion when we left Brownwood. We were the Service and Ammunition Battery of the Second Battalion of the 131st Field Artillery. We arrived in Honolulu December 1, and we left on the second. I was having a late breakfast on ship when the announcement came that Pearl Harbor had been bombed by the Japanese on December 7. We were now at war. We learned that we would be turning further south from our northwest movement. We stopped at Suva in Fiji and then landed in Brisbane, Australia on December 22. Just before the New Year, we left on the *Bloemfontein*, a new Dutch ship. We traveled north from Brisbane and met a convoy going to the Strait of Celebes. We turned around and traveled back to Surabaya in Java. At Malang we were quartered at a Dutch army airport where we provided cookhouse and munitions loading support to the 18th Bombardment Group. The Japanese began bombing the Malang Airport February 3, 1942. We were practically the only defense there. We had two service battery trucks firing 50 caliber weapons. There were three of us—Sgt. H.J. Whatley from Lubbock, and Pvt. Wesley Joyce Hoch, and myself. We shot down two planes. Strafers came in a couple of waves, and then their bombers, which they used to destroy the aircraft at the Dutch base. We pulled seven planes out of fires with winch trucks," Martinez recalled.

"The Japanese had spies on the island. On the radio, Tokyo Rose named over a dozen people close to us. She would say our wives and our girlfriends were playing around with our commanding officers. She played better music than our armed forces radio. There were 635 of us on Java, which was the entire complement of the Battalion, and 15,000 Australians and Englishmen, and 45,000 Dutch. We went from Batavia to Serang on the eastern coast overlooking the straits between Sumatra and Java where the U.S.S. *Houston* had been sunk the night of February 29. Java was hit in three places by 60,000 Japanese troops. We split with E Battery, the one that Max Offerle, another Laredoan, was in. The Dutch, all of them, surrendered. Battalion Cmdr. Col. Tharp said that he was going to surrender with the sick and wounded. He told us that anyone who wanted to keep fighting could take whatever they wanted. Thirty-six of us took a 1942 Plymouth staff car, a Jeep, a truck, and a trailer. We wanted to cut a path through the barbed wire to the let the Australian troops attack a block house. I was at the rear of the group. Everyone who was with me is dead. Only four or five men of the 150 who split off are now alive. We lost so few in combat, but lost 32% in the Japanese camp," Martinez said.

"I was captured June 8. I was loaded down with bolt cutters, a heavy Browning automatic rifle, ammo, a pistol, and two canteens when I came to a place over which I had to jump. My leggings caught in concertina wire and dragged the wire with me until I fell into the barbed wire. One man captured me. He cut me loose with my own bolt cutters. I had wire cuts to my face, arms, back, and shoulders. I would find out years later that there were shattered pieces

Though he was loathe to hear himself called a hero, the heroics of Sgt. Homero Martinez were legendary and an inspiration to Laredoans of all ages. The dapper, erudite Martinez who survived the deprivations of Japanese prisoner of war camps, died December 30, 2000.

COURTESY OF ALICIA MARTINEZ

of bone in some of my wounds. The Japanese sent me to a British camp at Batavia (now Djakarta). They had us loading ships with things they were stealing—gold, appliances, and refrigerators," he said.

"The Japanese took us to the Bicycle Camp inside Batavia, a military camp where the Dutch Bicycle Troops were prisoners. The Korean soldiers who looked after us were at the bottom of the rung, and they treated us like they were treated by the Japanese, with slaps and kicks. They beat you for any reason. When one of them broke my arm with a rifle stock, a Dutch doctor, Dr. Hendrik Hekking, set it with bamboo splints. In the camp we came down with illnesses we had never heard of, including Malaria, Dengue fever, black water fever, two types of dysentery, and tropical ulcers. Dr. Hekking saved my life twice. He would trade his medical services to Japanese soldiers with venereal disease for medicines he needed to treat us," Martinez recalled.

"We Americans were used for specialty jobs, like distributing supplies and rations for those who were building the railroad across Burma. We ran odd jobs up and down the railroad from Mouelmein, Burma to Bangkok, Thailand. The railroad was being built by native laborers, Chinese laborers, Malaysians, the British, Dutch, Australians, and New Zealanders. There were surveyors, diggers filling in the roadway, stone cutters making the railroad bed, shovel and pick men cutting passage through the mountains, a crew laying in the ties. The native and Chinese laborers were fed what the rest of us prisoners were fed—rice from the floor sweepings that included rat dung. The railroad would be a fulfillment of the Japanese dream of a Greater Asia, Asia Raya, a Malayan term for the conquest of Mongolians, Koreans, Chinese, Malaysians, and Indians. Some of the Japanese officers who were construction engineers had not been home since 1936," he said.

"Near the end, we could tell the tide had turned. We had become such a large liability to them. We demanded a great deal of their energy. Our Korean guards could hardly disguise their hate for the Japanese. We were sent to dig caves at Na Kon Na Yok. I now weighed 93 pounds and would not have lasted 45 more days. I had Malaria, tropical ulcers, and stone bruises. Thank God the bomb was dropped and that the Japanese finally surrendered. We were picked up by a Major in a commando group who took us to warehouses on the wharves of Bangkok," Martinez said.

"We were given new uniforms, food, and medical attention," Martinez said, and even now, 54 years later, there is such a measure of gratitude in his voice for the care he received. "The doctor said, 'You're in a hell of a shape.'"

Martinez was flown to an American hospital in Calcutta. "We were feted with a superlative banquet of every kind of food. It just made us sick, though, because our stomachs had shrunk from starvation. We got better, a little stronger. The PX was turned over to us. We could have whatever we wanted. Captain Taylor from Waco told me I would be leaving by air for Washington, D.C. I had been helping him prepare documents for the Pentagon about where the dead were buried, what were the atrocities. At the airport in Washington, I ran into a slim version of Edmundo Rendon, the son of the tailors on Lincoln Street in Laredo. It was quite a reunion. I stayed at Walter Reed Hospital while in Washington, and then I came south on a troop train to New Orleans and then to San Antonio. I ran into Roberto Azios in front of the Gunter Hotel in San Antonio, and he brought me home," Martinez continued.

"I came home to a family who had never believed I was dead," Martinez said of his parents, Margarito Martinez García and María de Jesus Hernández de Martinez. "The government had reported me 'captured in action, believed dead,' and offered them my insurance money," he said.

In those last moments of an interview that could have ended at several places prior, Homero Martinez lingered over bits of conversation, clarifying this or that detail. He said, "I had done the damnedest things to stay alive, using the trapping skills I had learned as a boy on a ranch—catching monkeys, dogs, iguanas, snakes. The battle became not the war, but the battle to stay alive."

The Terrible Business of War

"I left Laredo by train on October 12, 1942 with Daniel Salinas and Ciro Martinez," recalled U.S. Army Air Corps gunner José María Guerra. "We reported to our recruiter in San Antonio and then traveled to Wichita Falls. It had been 85° in Laredo when we left. When we got to Wichita, it had been sleeting and was 22°," he continued.

"Though they said they would keep us together, they split us up pretty quickly. I ended up in Oklahoma City and entered a one-year flight cadet program. We took military flight classes in single engine planes. I soloed in an Aereonca closed cockpit, single engine prop plane. The flight cadet program was very aggressive and strict about comportment and dress. After about nine months, we were sent to California for another round of tests to see how well suited we were to flying. A flaw in my depth perception kept me from piloting, but it did not keep me from being a crew member," Guerra said.

"We went to armor school in Denver to learn everything about the machine guns on B-24s. We were then sent to the gunnery school at Laredo Air Field for four months to fly and fire from AT-6 trainers at a decoy plane pulling a wind sock target. We honed our marksmanship skills on the ground with 12 gauge shotguns and clay targets. We were also building up our physical stamina with running and calisthenics. Ismael Montalvo was our coach," Guerra recalled.

"We shipped out to California and then to Tonopah, Nevada, which is where we took our B-24 training. We had now formed into a 10-man crew. We agreed that we would rotate the turret position, which was the hardest of positions because you had to fit yourself upside down into a very small hatch that screwed down and was lowered hydraulically. We flew practice runs to San Francisco and Los Angeles, and after 30 days shipped out from Hamilton Field by troop train to New Jersey. It took us three days. I remember the coal exhaust and the coal dust from that trip. We boarded a troop ship to cross the Atlantic. The ship was filled with bunks, eight bunks high. It carried thousands of us. It took us five days to cross the Atlantic in a convoy. We were flanked by supply ships, destroyers, and submarines. The convoy tacked across the sea to keep from being a target for enemy submarines," he said.

"We docked in southern England, and were then sent to Tibenham, a very small town that was the B-24 base for the 8th Air Force. The 8th Air Force was two-thirds B-17s and one-third B-24s. We were sent to a small town in Ireland for 10 days to learn from gunners who had combat experience. They were so elated to be back and finished. We returned to Tibenham to prepare. There was not a great deal of information from the officers about how the war was going. We read the London newspapers and sometimes listened to Axis Sally on the German propaganda radio station. She would tell you how many of our planes had been shot down and name the men on those planes. We believed we were winning the war," he said.

"There were 32 planes in service at Tibenham. We lived in Quonset huts filled with folding metal cots, a door at each end, and a coal heater. We were awakened each morning at 3 a.m., fed breakfast, and then briefed. A red string on a map of Europe told you where you were going on that mission. We went to the planes and started them, checked the guns, and prepared to take off. Our first strike was about 600 miles away in Dessau, Germany, a refining town. We flew off in formation, two B-24s on our right, but stepped down from each other. We were the third plane in the step. At Dessau, the topmost plane was hit by flak. It went down and hit the second plane. A ball of fire of both planes shooting out empty parachutes was coming to us and would have hit us except that it exploded in the air. We flew through the wreckage of that explosion. I was in the tail and could only hear by radio what had happened. No one survived. Twenty men who had been with us in the mess hall that morning were gone," Guerra continued.

"There was a crew of Mexican airmen from New York who didn't speak Spanish. I used to

B-24 armor gunner Sgt. José María Guerra of the U.S. Army Air Corps flew 35 missions over Germany out of a base at Tibenham, England. He was a member of a 10-man crew, one of 37 crews that flew from Tibenham to thwart Nazi aggressions.

COURTESY OF JOSÉ MARÍA GUERRA

read them their letters from their mothers and grandmothers. They were cocky men, full of bravado, the way young men are. They didn't come to chapel like the rest of us to pray or take Communion every morning. One who spoke for the rest said, 'If it was your time to go, it was your time, and prayer wouldn't intervene.' On their first mission out, they lost a crew member. They came to chapel after that. They became believers. On their seventh or eighth mission out, they were all killed. It was very hard to look at their empty beds and to prepare their personal effects which would be sent to their families," Guerra said. "The sight of their empty cots and having to prepare their possessions, the finality of it, this converted into men whoever of us were still boys."

Guerra completed 35 air missions over Germany, the last on February 14, 1945 over Madenburg. He was decorated with seven Air Medals and five Battle Stars for service in Northern France, Rhineland, Ardennes, and the Battle of the Bulge. He also received a Presidential Unit Citation. He had spent 36 months in the service, 18 in combat.

Guerra recalled the trip home from war. "We came home on the Queen Mary, docking in New York on April 12, 1945. The war was not behind us. The well and the living were on the topmost decks. The wounded were carried below. I came to Laredo by train, thinking all the way home that the life I lived before 1942 was not the life I lived now."

"The first thing I did when I got home was to ask my prospective mother-in-law for Amanda's hand," he said. José Guerra married Amanda Gutierrez on April 16, 1945.

In 1967, he was appointed by President Lyndon Johnson to serve on the Selective Service Draft Board. He served until 1976.

From a Journal of War

I would hope that this gives my grandsons and granddaughters an idea of what the war was, what war is. There is no way that a person can rationalize that war is dramatic or heroic or beneficial or necessary. War is a terrible business, attested to by those who can no longer speak, by the wounded and maimed, by those who lost a loved one, by those who know their lifespan has been considerably shortened by experiences under fire and stress, both physical and emotional.

Long after actual combat—whether it was on land or at sea or in the air—there endures the sharpness of the ordeal an absolute appreciation for the wonder of life itself. I have a very special thankfulness for the colors of the sky, the textures of the greenery, and above all that my life was spared in war to enjoy the blessings of a family such as I have of my wife and five children.

The stress of combat so many years ago allows me not to press the panic button when a problem presents itself, as though the war gave me a sense of value to differentiate the important from the not-so-important.

There are some who wail over what was destroyed in the American and British bombing of historic Dresden—cathedrals, castles, the wall of the city. It was terrible, the way war is, but it should be remembered that German air power destroyed much of London, including churches, schools, cathedrals, and thousands of Londoners. During the Battle of Britain, the English had to resort to sending many of the children of southern England to northern England to save them. This was a heartbreaking blow to many families.

I was in England at this time. After the Germans lost the Battle of Britain, they started a bombardment directed at London with pilotless planes with buzz bombs and only enough fuel to reach London. The Germans also perfected the use of rockets to firebomb London.

English civilians—men, women, and children—would fill the subway system at night to be safe from the nightly bombardment.

On a mission to Kassel, Germany, we were hit by flak and lost an engine. The flak had torn a hole in one of our wing rubber gas tanks. Gasoline sprayed throughout the plane. We saw flame exhaust coming from one of the engines a few feet away from the stream of gasoline.

We turned off our heated suits, the intercom, the radio, anything to prevent a spark. After five minutes, the gasoline emptied from the ruptured tank. Another five minutes and the fumes and gas had evaporated. The lack of power caused us to fly out of formation. German fighter planes loved to wait for bomber stragglers. They would line up and take turns at the stragglers. We needed to get back to England. Over an open field we dropped all our bombs. We were flying at about 50 feet to get away from the

German fighters. Another engine went out and we started pitching out ammunition, flak suits, parachutes, and anything that was not bolted to the plane. We were so low over the English Channel that we were leaving wake over the water. We dismounted ten 50-caliber guns and pitched them overboard. We gained another 25 feet of altitude, trying to make landfall. A British airbase gave us instructions for landing. We had dinner with the British and spent the night, a very cold night at their base. They apologized for the lack of coal for heating but said that most of the coal in England went to American bases.

I was the gunner and armorer of our crew. I flew in the nose turret, top turret, tail turret, and either left or right waist window of the B-24. My duties included taking care of the 50-caliber machine guns and arming bombs after take-off. If the mission was aborted for any reason, I had to disarm the bombs for a safe landing at our base in England.

Each bomb had a four-inch propeller on the nose, held in place by a safety wire. I armed the bombs by removing the wire. When the bomb was dropped, the wind would unscrew the propeller. Bombs were held in the bomb bays by two pincers and two lugs. When the pincers were activated electrically by the bombardier, the pincers released the bombs.

On one particular mission, approaching Hamburg on a clear day, I could see the intense flak and that some of our bombers had been hit and went down. We completed our mission and made it away from the German flak and were headed back when the bombardier called me on the interphone to say that one of the bomb lights was on, that a bomb had not gone out, that the bomb bays were open. I disconnected myself from the plane's oxygen system, from the interphone, and from the heating system that went into our suits. I grabbed a five-minute oxygen bottle and a large screwdriver and went into the bomb bay, walking over the eight-inch catwalk. I took off my parachute to make it into the tight space. It was 40 ° below, maybe colder with the wind coming up through the open bay. I saw the hanging bomb. The back lug was held by the pincers, the front lug released. The propeller was gone and the bomb was armed. My oxygen bottle said I had three-and-a-half minutes left, which made me try harder and faster. The pincer wouldn't open up enough. I had a minute-and-a-half of oxygen left. I did what I had to do, I kicked it very carefully three times and the bomb dropped. I barely made it back to my oxygen and heating connections and to my parachute.

I wonder if God intervened on my behalf that day, thinking perhaps I was too young to die or that the other nine members of the crew were not deserving to die in this way.

There are some things you remember more than others. Axis Sally on German radio had a mission to demoralize us. She played all the latest American hits and in-between she told us who had been shot down from the 8th Air Force. She told us that while we were overseas that the Jews and the Zoot Suiters were taking our girls and our wives. She called President Roosevelt Rosenfelt and said he was a Jew being ordered about by Jews. She played Bing Crosby's music and called him Herr Bingle. Her words were full of hate and were meant to hurt us.

I remember the visit from Col. Jimmy Stewart, the actor who had led a number of the first missions of the Battle of the Bulge. He came to our base on December 23, 1944. We had been grounded by sleet and bad weather. Col. Stewart said things were going dangerously bad at the Battle of the Bulge. He came to ask for volunteers to fly, despite the bad weather. Thirty B-24 crews volunteered, one of which crashed at take-off, killing all 10 members of the crew. The next day, Col. Stewart flew in the lead B-24 and for the next four or five days we flew every day in support of the ground troops, bombing German tanks at the Battle of the Bulge.

We were de-briefed after each mission and then visited by the flight surgeon who had a bottle of Scotch with him. We each had a shot, a double since half of the crew did not drink. We had had our breakfast 12 hours earlier. We had been on oxygen six or seven hours. The Scotch went straight to our heads.

The ten of us crew members were like brothers. What hurt one made us all bleed. One of our crew members would become violently ill with airsickness. He refused to be grounded, though the flight surgeon wanted this. We looked out for him, making sure he was on oxygen and that his heated suit was on. His struggle to remain part of our crew kept us together tightly. He made us believe it was one for all and

❖

Above: Four days after docking in New York on April 12, 1945, José Guerra married Amanda Gutierrez in Laredo.

Below: Sgt. Guerra trained at Laredo Air Field and bases in Oklahoma City and Tonopah, Nevada. By the time World War II had come to its conclusion, he had been decorated with seven Air Medals, Five Battle Stars, and a Presidential Unit Citation for service in Northern France, Rhineland, Ardennes, and the Battle of the Bulge.

COURTESY OF JOSÉ MARÍA GUERRA

Above, left: President of the Selective Service Draft Board Guerra gives the oath of office to Edward Lightner. Appointed by President Lyndon B. Johnson in 1967, Guerra served with Richard Buitron, Guadalupe Martinez, Fernando Vela, and Arturo Benavides.

COURTESY OF JOSÉ MARÍA GUERRA

Below, right: Frank X. Leyendecker joined the U.S. Navy just before his 18th birthday, seeing service during World War II in Okinawa and Yokohama.

COURTESY OF ELIZABETH LEYENDECKER

Below: Leyendecker carried with him throughout the war this photograph of his mother, Emma Jordan Leyendecker, who died just after his return in 1946.

COURTESY OF FRANK X. LEYENDECKER

all for one. He completed 35 missions with us. His name was John J. Werdell from Los Angeles.

Our crew had been formed in Tonapah, Nevada in 1943. We knew each other well. We would travel on leave from Tonapah to Los Angeles and on one of our excursions we stopped in the middle of the night at a restaurant, finding a table that seated the 10 of us. Then, my crew members rose abruptly and filed out, none of them speaking. I followed them and got back in the rented car. One of the crew members pointed me to a sign on a bench as we drove off. The sign read, "No dogs or Mexicans allowed."

These are the things I remember about being a young man in the war.

—José M. Guerra

A REMEMBRANCE OF WAR

"Our serial numbers were contiguous," Frank X. Leyendecker remembers of joining the Navy with fellow Laredoans Jimmy Gallagher and Richard Ortiz.

Leyendecker joined in 1944 just before his 18th birthday and traveled to boot camp on a troop train to San Diego with Gallagher and Ortiz. "One of our instructors was Freddie Peña. We seemed to run into people from Laredo wherever we were," he recalled. "The purpose of boot camp was to tear all your thinking apart and discipline you so that you would learn to make every minute and every action count."

After five weeks in San Diego, Leyendecker came home briefly before reporting to San Bruno, California to learn how to handle small boats and landing craft. "We traveled after that on the U.S.S. *Lagrange*, a troop carrier of 2,300 men, to Okinawa. The men who manned the *Lagrange* had been in combat before. They sort of prepared us emotionally for all that we didn't know about what we would experience. That was something, not knowing what was going to happen. You were trained. You wanted to come through all of this without any scratches. You prayed a little harder. We were sent there to mop up the island which had been invaded a few weeks before. The war was winding down. We were met with strafing," Leyendecker said. "So much of Okinawa was still beautiful, even though it had been devastated," he said.

"My good friend Roberto Volpe had been killed in Okinawa. I found his grave and shaved off a sliver of wood from the cross that marked his burial. I brought it to his mother as well a picture of Roberto's grave. The war was devastating to all of our mothers. At one time, my mother had four sons in the war. She wrote to me all the time, and I missed her. I carried her picture with me. It never left me, and neither did her words or her love," Leyendecker said, reading the inscription on the back of a water stained photo of Emma Jordan Leyendecker that remained in his wallet throughout the war. A simple inscription reads, "To my beloved son, Mother."

"All of us served," Leyendecker said, naming his brothers, "Albert, Dick, Sam, Gilbert, Peter,

and me, four at once in World War II, two of us in Korea," he said.

"Some of the Japanese were terrified of the American soldiers after the war ended. Rather than surrender, some of them threw themselves off the high cliffs at Okinawa," he recalled.

"In 1946 I went to Yokohama. To this day I have a very vivid memory of something I saw there. A few days before reaching land, the ship's garbage doesn't go into the water. It gets stored. We had plenty of it before reaching Yokohama. We docked and tied up there. We weren't allowed off the ship. We were taking on troops. What I remember so clearly is Japanese civilians going up the ship's ropes to find something to eat in our garbage," he said.

"I lost my mother right after I got back. She died in 1946. I think the stress of having all her sons in the service got to her. It affected all of us. You grew up overnight. The experiences of those years are inside all of us. They hardly ever surface, but they do. I still think of those desolate and remote cliffs where the Japanese jumped off rather than face their captors. You'd think all these years later that those memories would dissipate. We came back street-wise, full of new lessons. If my innocence was all I lost, I was lucky," Leyendecker said.

Boat Swain's Mate Second Class Leyendecker was 19 when he was discharged on July 4, 1946. "A troop train took us from San Diego to Galveston. I came home to join the family business, City Lumber. I stayed in the reserves and was called to the Korean War in 1950. I reported to Houston and went to orientation in San Diego and then to Treasure Island near San Francisco," he said.

"I made 13 trips to Alaska on a tanker that delivered jet fuel. It was always an adventure on very turbulent waters. It was beautiful. You couldn't fill your eyes enough with the beauty of it, the whales at St. Lawrence, the porpoises escorting the ships. Standing watch at night, you would ask, 'What am I doing here? Will I ever get home?' I prayed that I would," Leyendecker said.

"World War II veterans came home to a grateful nation. They tell their stories with pride and they are selfless. They did not whine. The wars since then have been different. I believe in my country, and I'm proud I served. I think about those years, though, the years of my life that were put on hold, the years a young man should be making his luck and his life," he said softly, feeling the weight of memory.

"War destroys more than men. It destroys the souls of men and whole landscapes and families. Wars are fought over imaginary lines and parallels. It was two wars, two sets of experiences that I went through. I was on the fringes of it, but I saw enough of it to know I wouldn't want my children or grandchildren to have the same experiences," he said.

One of Millions: A Holocaust Survivor's Story

David Sanitzki has lived in Laredo since Labor Day weekend 1974, when he moved from Valley Stream, Long Island where he had lived since emigrating from Germany in March 1950. His demeanor is that of a man younger than his 74 years, buoyant and talkative. One wouldn't imagine that he spent the entirety of World War II—the entirety of his boyhood—imprisoned by the Nazis in nearly a dozen concentration camps, but the faded blue numerals tattooed on his forearm bear sobering witness to the horror of the Holocaust that consumed six million Jews as well as millions of Roma (Gypsies), handicapped, Slavic peoples (Poles, Russians, and others), homosexuals, Jehovah's Witnesses, Free Masons, political dissidents, Communists, and Socialists.

When the Nazis invaded Poland in 1939, Sanitzki was 14 and living in the town of Zychlin, where he was born, some 80 kilometers from Warsaw. Once the Nazis occupied Zychlin, they proceeded to pull Jewish men and youths from their homes and press them into forced labor gangs. Sanitzki was among these laborers. He and his eldest brother Nathan were taken to Wizengrunt, a work camp across the Polish border in Germany. "I was a big strong boy, but they didn't see me as a boy," Sanitzki said of the Nazis, "they saw me as a man."

Sanitzki was at Wizengrunt for about six weeks when they took Nathan away to work. Sanitzki was ill at the time and so was left behind.

A Nazi commander called the Tiger came for the prisoners at Wizengrunt and marched them to Roksn, another camp about 20 kilometers away. Wizengrunt, Roksn, and other camps in the area were work camps. The prisoners were used to build roads. The overseers, Sanitzki said, "were very bad people. They used to beat us with shovels, sticks, anything. You couldn't take a shower," Sanitzki said. "The lice ate you. There were a lot of lice because it was cold and there was no place to bathe or wash yourself." Sanitzki spent about another six weeks at Roksn before being moved to Bretz, another work camp, and then to Witenberger in 1940.

At Witenberger the prisoners were used to construct buildings and build railroads. "We had to carry two sacks of cement at one time," Sanitzki said, "up on the third floor, the fourth floor of what they were building. A 12-foot rail we had to carry with two people."

The routine and Sanitzki's internment at Witenberger lasted for one and a half years. This was the time before the pace of the extermination of the Jews quickened, though it was nevertheless carried out. The forced labor pool for the Nazis was at this point apparently too valuable to utterly destroy, though there was not much concern given the laborers who suffered and died from exhaustion and maltreatment.

In 1943 there came an order. "It was around June or July, something like that, very hot," Sanitzki said. He was now 18 years old. "I remember I fell in one of the [railroad] cars what we were working—unloading it—and I fainted because of the heat and no food. But after a while, they sent us away to Birkenau."

Auschwitz-Birkenau was one of the six killing sites in Poland—along with Belzec, Sobibor, Treblinka, Chelmno, and Majdanek—chosen for that purpose because of their proximity to rail lines and location in semi-rural areas. The largest number of European Jews and Gypsies were killed there during the war—1.25 million, ninety percent of which were Jews.

"But we were lucky when we came to Birkenau," Sanitzki said, "because one of the S.S. sent a letter along with us that we were very good workers, we were very hard workers, and we could be used there. We were in Birkenau maybe a week or so.

"Birkenau was [a camp] where you just passed through," Sanitzki continued. "And then they took you to Auschwitz. In Auschwitz they decided what to do with you. So when they started putting numbers on you, then you knew that you were going to be alive.

"I worked on building the street from Birkenau to Auschwitz. When I was working on that road, there were two different kinds of people. There were Polish people—Christians—and Jewish people. Two groups.

"And then after a while, Mengele came to the camp."

Josef Mengele was known as the Angel of Death in the camps, one of the most infamous Nazis associated with the Holocaust.

"All of us had to fall in," Sanitzki said, "and Mengele started looking over everybody. I was standing with a friend. The friend was standing in front of me; we used to go to school together. When he came up to Mengele, Mengele looked at him. He showed him his hands. And then he put him to the left. Putting to the left we knew we remained in camp. And when I came up to him, he looked at my hands and my body, because we were naked in front of him, and he put me to the right. And I said to him, 'Why are you putting me to the right and him to the left? We're the same age. He's my friend, I would like to be with him.' So he pushed me over to the left. He wouldn't answer, but he pushed me over to the left. So I just went over. After that, when he picked up so many people, I think it was about 500 or 600 people, he sent us to Goleszof."

Goleszof was in Poland, located near a quarry at Schteinbruch where the inmates would dynamite and pick stone for a brick and cement factory. Sanitzki remained there until the beginning of 1944.

"Then, all of a sudden, they started liquidating Goleszof," Sanitzki said.

By this time the war had turned against Germany. The Allied armies approached German territory by late 1944, and the S.S. began speeding up the extermination of prisoners or evacuating the outlying concentration camps. The Nazis began deporting prisoners to camps inside Germany to prevent their liberation and to hide the evidence of the genocide.

"It was in January, I remember, and my uncle was in there, my mother's younger brother was there, and we started marching toward Glaivz," Sanitzki said. "It was a long, long march. I fell down because we were wearing wooden shoes, and the snow pasted itself into the wood. So my uncle and friend of mine grabbed me under my arms and they pulled me along because it was not far from Glaivz. It wasn't where to stay, it was only a pig house, they kept pigs in there with water. We found some stones we put stones in the water, then we took off the doors and put them on the stones, and that's where we slept.

"In the morning they loaded us up in freight-cars. It was snowing, cold, freezing. They took us from there to Oranienburg. They undressed us completely, and we stood in the freezing weather outside for about six hours, I guess. Then they gave us hot shower. They tried to kill us either way, the best way they could, but they couldn't make it. We were young, we were strong. From there they sent us to Flosenburg."

Flosenburg was the site of a hangar. "They had straw on the floor," Sanitzki said. "That's where we slept. We were there about two weeks, I guess. After that, they made groups and they split us up. I went to Platling, and we were working there at the airport." It was early 1945.

"The American planes came," Sanitzki said. "At the airport there were 145 Messerschmidts—German planes, fighters—and they shot them all up. Every plane was on fire. I remember one German was running, and one of the bullets took off his leg. Then the Germans lay down and we had to lay down on them to cover them. But when we saw all the planes on fire, then we got up, and we took off the jackets, the striped jackets from the concentration camps, and we were waving to the pilots. They were very close to us, they looked at us. But they didn't touch us."

Fifty-four years have passed since that moment, but it is one that still causes Sanitzki to pause when speaking of it. The power of the memory overwhelms him.

"They went away," Sanitzki continued. "After that, the camp was liquidated, and we started going towards Austria. They had there some kind of place, I don't remember, where they killed the rest of the people. While we were walking, we came into a city called Vaging, and we stayed there overnight in a pig house. They always found pig houses.

"In the morning we walked out of Vaging—it was May, May 4, I think—and it was snowing terrible, and while we were walking the snow stopped. And then all of a sudden we saw the German army coming along. In the front was some kind of officer, must have been a general or something, and he stopped the car, and he said to the S.S.—" [At this point, Sanitzki spoke a German phrase, then said, "I don't want to say it in English."] "'Who is that?' And they said, 'This is from concentration camp.' And he said to them, 'The Russians are in the back and the Americans are in the front, and you're going with them?' So they started ripping off their S.S. marks, and they said to us, 'Either you're leaving, or we have to kill you. Whatever you want. Split up and run wherever you want.'" So we split up in groups of three or four friends, and we came back into the city, to Vaging."

Nazi concentration camp survivor David Sanitzki pictured with his wife, Oona in New York. Sanitzki was interned at Auschwitz-Birekneau, one of six Nazi killing sites.

COURTESY OF DAVID SANITZKI

A farmer let Sanitzki and his companions stay in his barn and fed them. "In the morning, one of our friends—there were three of us—looked out, and he saw white flags, and he says, 'We're all free. The war is over.'"

In the chaos of post-war Europe, re-establishing contact with displaced friends and family was a monumental task, more so for survivors of the camps, any records of whose relatives were destroyed. But doing so was not impossible. Sanitkzi heard of his brother's survival through friends. "Everything through friends, mouth to mouth," Sanitzki said.

"The Army left to Paris, and from Paris they went home, so I decided to go to Germany. That's when I met my brother. I stayed in Germany until I came to United States, on March 11, 1950 on the ship the *General Hershey*."

❖

David Sanitzki met up after World War II with his brothers Aaron and Al. The Sanitzki brothers lost their parents Paula and Joseph, and baby sister Manya to the Nazis.

COURTESY OF DAVID SANITZKI

During his stay at one of the camps, the Germans gave the prisoners soup made from the fat of pigs they killed for food. The soup soon spoiled, but the Nazis continued to feed it to the prisoners. "Everybody got diarrhea," Sanitzki said. "Everyday that's all they gave us. They tried to kill us every which way. Some of them died from it. I was in the hospital maybe six weeks."

Sanitzki was treated by a Polish doctor who was in the camp as a political prisoner. "The doctor said to me in Polish, 'David, you got a heart from a horse. If you survive this....' Because he said, 'I can only give you one aspirin a day.' For typhus, one aspirin in a day is no medicine." Thoughts of his mother gave Sanitzki the will to hang on. "And God was there with me all the time. And I did come out of it," he said quietly. "I did come out of it."

"A friend of mine was working in the kitchen and he kept me alive," Sanitzki continued. "His name was Pinkus. He kept me alive. Because otherwise, if not for him, I would have been killed in the hospital." Prisoners in the hospital who grew increasingly more ill were taken to the hospital's attic. The camp boss would make periodic visits to the attic, where he choked the ailing prisoners to death by stepping on their throats. Through the haze of his illness, Sanitkzi overheard the camp boss tell the doctor that Sanitzki would probably be sent to the attic himself soon. "It was like my mother said, 'Wake up and listen.' And I sent for Pinkus. Pinkus came up and I told him and then I fell back asleep. And Pinkus made the doctor leave me there in the hospital: 'This is my brother. You want to kill my brother? I'm gonna kill you, I'm not gonna give you any food.' Because he cooked for him. So he said, 'I didn't know it's your brother.' That's how I'm alive. And I never could find Pinkus, never. I always think about him but I could never find him."

"There's a lot of things like this. There's a lot to talk about. You gotta sit, and keep on and keep and keep on.... You get choked up with certain items. Like my sister. She was 11 years old. A little girl. A tiny little girl. A thin, thin little girl. She was the apple of our eye. We were three brothers and one sister. She was the youngest one.

"She used to write me letters to the camp," Sanitzki said. "I remember she used to write me. I'll never forget that. I remember: 'Keep yourself clean. Cleanliness is health.' An 11 year-old kid."

When the letters stopped coming, Sanitzi knew his parents, Paula and Joseph, and sister, Manya, were gone. It was an occurrence common in the camp: the fragile link to family was broken "when you didn't get any letters. You didn't get any information from home. You wrote home," Sanitzki said. "It came back because there was nobody there no more. And that's how you know. And through other people that they notified, that this-and-this city was liquidated, this-and-this city was gone to Treblinka. And when we got the letter that Zychlin—the ghetto—was all liquidated, they went to Treblinka, I knew. You didn't know what date. You didn't know. But you knew that's where they were killed."

But his brothers had survived. Sanitzki found Aaron in Garmish after the war, as noted earlier. The middle brother, he had worked for the German mayor of Zychlin building a mayor's palace in town. His friend was a bricklayer and took Al along as a helper, and they worked on the building until sometime in 1941 or 1942. He was sent from there to work at a farm estate for a time with other young Jewish men and women before being relocated once again, this time to a concentration camp. "Because they worked in a place like this, they were stronger," Sanitzki said. "They had more food, they got food regularly. Then afterward they gave everything back through the nose when they went to the camp." Late in the war, during a prisoner relocation by train, Al was able to escape, and was hidden in a basement by a German civilian for a few days until the train had left. "They didn't count any more at that time," Sanitzki said. "They left the train open, and people would run. Whoever wanted to run away was running." Al lived in Germany until 1949 when he came to the United States. Sanitzki's oldest brother Nathan made his way to Belgium and then came to the United States.

"It's not imaginable," Sanitzki said. "Even myself. But this is what happened to me. I was at the time 16 years old, 17 years old. I was still a boy. I grew up without my parents. I grew up on my own.

"Sometimes I get up in the morning, and I say to my wife, 'I had a very bad night.' It's already fifty years, more than fifty years. She says, 'What's wrong now?' I said, 'I was running, and they were chasing me. I couldn't catch my breath and I was running and they were right behind me but they couldn't catch me. And I was running and I was running and I was running....' And the rest of the night is shot, finished."

The dreams and the memories are all that remain of that time for Sanitzki. From before the war, there are no physical mementos. "I was too young," he said. "Who had time to think about things? Everything was burned. No birth certificates, no pictures. Nothing. The Germans burned everything."

Sanitzki sighed. "But I'm here in America and I'm a very happy man, especially here in Laredo. People are nice, I live in a nice neighborhood. What can I tell you?"

—Tom Moore

After Vietnam: A World Asking Us to Re-weave the Tapestry That Holds Us Together

"We came from an era in which we were told that we could make this a better world, and we believed it. The war in Vietnam did not make this a better world. It was a waste of lives and that waste lives with us now in lives ruined by injuries, disease, heroin addiction, and deep psychological scars," said Dr. Reynaldo Godines who served in Vietnam from June 1967 to October 1968.

❖

Reynaldo Godines, now a Laredo physician, believes Vietnam was "not a good war, a war that cost this country 58,000 of its best and brightest young men and women." Godines said that Vietnam was waged by the military industrial complex at a cost of the equivalent of a trillion dollars today. He believes that the Vietnam War was layered with conspiracies including the assasination of President John F. Kennedy.

DR. REYNALDO GODINES

"Don't write this unless you make mention of President Kennedy's NSAM #263 (National Security Action Memorandum) of October 11, 1963, which would have returned all U.S. personnel from Vietnam by the end of 1965. NSAM #263 is one of the 'whys' of the Kennedy assassination, according to L. Fletcher Prouty," said Godines, who upon his return from Vietnam resumed his college studies.

"At the time that President John F. Kennedy was assassinated, the U.S. had spent one billion dollars on the war in Vietnam. During the LBJ and Nixon administrations, the government spent 200 billion dollars. By the end of the war, over 500 billion would have been spent. The government that wanted this war was a government away and apart from that of the people. It was run by then CIA director Allan Dulles and the military industrial complex of great proportions, which President Eisenhower warned us about in his farewell speech," he said.

"I had never heard of Vientam in high school," said Godines, noting that he had joined the Naval Reserve in the last half of his senior year, 1966, at Martin High School. "I started to hear about it while I was at Laredo Junior College. My friend Mundo, Edmundo Ramirez, and I were called to active duty at the same time. I flew from San Diego by commercial airline to Guam and then to Subic Bay. Even the airlines were enjoying the economic boon of wartime prosperity," Godines continued.

"Mundo went to the First Naval Infantry. The government was short of Marines and soldiers—they were dying too fast. Mundo was part of the firepower and he survived some of the worst hand-to-hand battles of the war. He saw it all—suicidal waves of Chinese and North Vietnamese soldiers doped and armed coming at you day and night. Mundo was a survivor," Godines said.

"I was a little luckier. I was at the lowest level of service, a deck ape on a tanker ship fueling American ships on the coast of Vietnam. This position was the first instance in which I experienced discrimination. It was assumed by my name that I was working at an assignment commensurate with my abilities. When I passed a test for advancement and it was noted that I had two semesters of college behind me, I became a petty officer," he recounted.

Godines was assigned to the U.S.S. *Rehobeth*, a high tech spy ship off the coast of North Vietnam. "You could smell death at night," he recalled. "In the distance you saw what you first believed to be lightning, but it was the land mass and mountains backlit by the explosions of air strikes. The *Rehobeth* was the sister ship of the U.S.S. *Pueblo*. When the *Pueblo* was captured, we had to leave North Vietnam immediately. The captors of the *Pueblo* now had our number, too," he recalled.

Godines returned stateside in October 1968. "Mundo came along in December 1968, and in January of the next year, both of us had enrolled at Laredo Community College. "In September 1969, I enrolled at the University of Texas. How we made it on $90 a month that the GI Bill allowed us is a mystery. Often, it wasn't enough. I finished at UT in two years," he said.

"Mundo transferred to Sam Houston State and ended up with a Masters in criminology," Godines said, and with such feeling for his best friend that it becomes clear that his life and Mundo's had been woven inextricably since their youth. "Mundo became a federal probation officer. He was shot through the heart in downtown Laredo in December 1975 by one of his parolees," Godines pauses a moment to feel what moves through his own heart. "We were best man at each other's weddings. Mundo had gone to the police department, the sheriff's department, and the FBI to ask for protection from the troubled parolee. They could offer no protection, but there is now a federal law to protect federal probation officers and law enforcement officers. Can you imagine surviving Vietnam and then being taken out of here by a crazy person? Such a waste," he said pointedly. "I remember Mundo all the time. There had been six of us who came from the neighborhood—me, Mundo, Roddy Applewhite, Quintin Vargas, Roberto Rios, and Gilberto Cardenas. We were in the first accelerated class at L.J. Christen. There were 24 students in that class, most of whose parents had not graduated from high school. Of the six of us who were close friends, we all went on with our education. Roddy is a Ph.D., a professor at the University of Houston. Quintin is Dr. Vargas, an administrator at St. Edward's University. Gilberto is Dr. Cardenas, a professor of economics at UT-Pan American. Roberto Rios is finishing work on a Ph.D. in mathematics," he said.

While at the University of Texas, Godines, earned a double major in biology and chemistry. He took part in the Freedom March against the war in Vietnam. "The Austin City Council and the University administration did all they could to keep the march from happening. I think 100,000 marched that day against the war. It wasn't so much a matter that I was against the war. It was that I believed I had earned the right by serving my country to have a voice, to speak up, to exercise my constitutional rights. It was that coupled with how I felt about Vietnam," Godines said.

"It was a not a good war. It was a war that the military industrial complex had been planning for. It was about protecting private interests and

Godines served on the high tech U.S.S. Rehobeth, *the sister ship of the U.S.S.* Pueblo. *"You could smell death at night," he said of his time in the waters off the coast of North Vietnam.*

DR. REYNALDO GODINES

making money, and at such great expense to the American people—58,000 young men and women taken from their families, a trillion dollars in 1999 dollars, the removal by violence of elected officials with high ideals that clashed with those of the military industrial complex, like President Kennedy and Robert Kennedy," he said. "Read *JFK, The CIA, Vietnam, and the Plot to Assassinate John F. Kennedy*. Read *Bloody Treason*. The explanations in those books for the war in Vietnam are day-and-night opposites for the reasons we thought we were in Vietnam when we were 19," Godines said.

"Not my children, not anyone's children. I don't want them to be exposed to any unnecessary war. There are more good people in the world than bad. According to our current CIA, the narcotic dollar is destroying global democracies. The military industrial complex has been replaced by a money laundering complex. Narcotic dollars fuel oppressive regimes, like Syria's. Narcotic dollars are destroying countries, continents, and lives. As humans, we have the ability to change how our government does business, to have a voice in its policies. As parents, we have the responsibility to raise good children who respect each other and who respect life, children who know that drugs are the ruin of lives. This world is asking us to be role models of respect and education. This world is asking us to re-weave the tapestry that holds us together, to make it grow, to allow us to live in peaceful co-existence," Godines said.

A Civilian in Vietnam

"There was danger everywhere," recalled José Cardona Martinez of his time in Vietnam as a civilian who worked for Lockheed to repair damaged aircraft. "Since the object of the enemy's focus was to destroy aircraft, including those I worked on, it seemed at times to me that I would not get out alive," he remembered.

"I saw it then, but could not say it then—Vietnam was a mess, a waste of human lives, resources, countries, hearts and lives. The idea that Americans and foreign troops would fight the Viet Cong in the jungle while the regular North Vietnamese and the regular army of South Vietnam would fight over the cities was a ridiculous idea. Why would you send an inexperienced G.I. to find the enemy in the jungle country of the enemy? That is why we lost so many men. I had worked at many bases repairing aircraft for return to combat, but I have never seen the level of incompetence and lack of heart that I saw in Vietnam. The people of South Vietnam did not want you there. Those who helped you in the day worked doubly hard at night to hurt you."

Martinez, who is known to his Catholic War Veteran contemporaries as "J.C." or "Lefty," was in Vietnam from April 1967 to March 1969.

"Saigon was under rocket fire when I got there. I was there for three months at Ben Hoa Air Force Base and then moved all over Vietnam—Tan Son Nhut, Chu Lai, Da Nang, Kan To," Martinez continued.

"We were targets. It wasn't a war. There was no front. It was guerrilla warfare," he said.

A civilian working for a defense contractor, Martinez wore a uniform but carried no weapon in Vietnam.

His career in the military began as a PFC in the United States Marine Corps. Martinez enlisted in 1946 and was assigned to VMR Marine Squadron 352 in Pearl Harbor. "We were part of a Marine Air Force service squadron. The C-54 was our airplane, a cargo and transport plane. We flew to different islands to take food and supplies," Martinez said. He was discharged June 13, 1947 and returned to his family in San Antonio. "I got

A 1967 map of South Vietnam.

my GED in 1947 and used the G.I. Bill to try my hand at college and business school. I ended up learning to fly at Maulding School of Aviation. I also learned everything I could about engines. I went to work for Slick Airways, an air freight company based out of San Antonio. I was a mechanic with a specialty in oxygen systems. Slick sent me to Burbank where I learned and specialized in sheet metal work and repair. I was a licensed mechanic, a crew chief, and an inspector," he said. Martinez returned to San Antonio and worked with Slick as an inspector and learned electroplating when the company diversified into that area. I ended up working for Slick for 10 years until Land Air recruited me for contract work for the Air Force in Europe and stateside. I worked in the Philippines as an inspector and then in Thailand as part of a State Department contract with the Royal Thai Air Force. Our job there was to upgrade 20 F-86 fighters. We worked seven days a week, 12 hours a day. We were in Vietnam briefly at a time during which there were only advisors in Vietnam and not troops," Martinez recalled.

J.C. "Lefty" Martinez enlisted in the service at the end of World War II and also saw service in Vietnam in 1967 and 1968 as a civilian working under contract to the Department of Defense.

COURTESY OF J.C. MARTINEZ

"I spent all of 1962 working on F-102s in Japan as a State Department inspector. I went to Okinawa in 1963 for six months working on the F-102s and then back to the Philippines and to Okinawa once again. When I came stateside to Sacramento, the company changed its organization and its name to Dynalectron Corporation. I worked on training planes there and then went to Hickham AFB in Honolulu," he said.

"When I came back to San Antonio in 1965, I went to work for Lockheed and was sent to Dover, Delaware as a chief inspector for the C-133s. The Air Force had built 50 of them and had lost 18 of them. They wanted to know why. It turned out they had been built in two different places with two different sets of blueprints that didn't match one to the other. We learned this only by tapping into all the systems of the C133. The plane was under-powered and weak in structure," Martinez continued.

"In 1965 I got an emergency call to work on 34 F-106s, fighters whose drag struts were breaking when they landed. We were now doing ultrasonic inspections without having to dismantle the planes. The planes were at Press Isle, Maine; Sault Saint Marie, MI; Mt. Clemens, MI; and Menault, North Dakota. It was then I learned of the opening in Japan, which eventually took me to Vietnam in 1967 for two of the longest years of my life."

La Política

War on Poverty

The War on Poverty and the advent of VISTA (Volunteers In Service to America) workers in Laredo in the mid-sixties fomented a rarely experienced politicization of Laredoans. Funded by the federal Office of Economic Opportunity, the War on Poverty and VISTA initiated a chain of events that would culminate late in the next decade with a great, heaving shift in the politics of this city.

The VISTAs arrived in Laredo in 1965. Recognized at first by the Old Party rule as benign interlopers who would help with educational and fix-up work in *barrio* homes, the volunteers created a flurry of activity in the city's oldest and poorest neighborhoods, organizing their leadership into councils that could chart improvements for the homes of *barrio* residents "The VISTAs made sure that the *barrio* residents fulfilled

❖

Political activist Chaca Ramirez.

JUAN RAMIREZ

Above: The corner of Salinas and Farragut was a hot-spot for protesters asking for minimum wage for cafe workers. While many townspeople shied away from participating in the protest, others supported it.

COURTESY OF JUAN RAMIREZ

Below: Governor Preston Smith heard the wishes of Laredoans who demanded a minimum wage. They are pictured at the Laredo International Bridge in 1968.

COURTESY OF JUAN RAMIREZ

the War on Poverty's proscribed 'maximum feasible representation' of the poor," said activist Luis Díaz De Leon who served as director of the Economic Opportunity Development Corporation (EODC) and later the Community Action Agency. The VISTAs who came here were from all over the country. "They were young, they questioned everything, and they had good intentions," Díaz De Leon recalled. "Some of them were conscientious objectors who could serve in this way instead of serving in the Vietnam war. We even got a young attorney just out of Stanford Law School. They were very visible across the community. Some of them organized tutorial and remedial classes, counseled dropouts, conducted a summer swimming program, and directed youth activities including Boy Scouts, Cub Scouts, and five 4-H Clubs. VISTA workers registered voters and taught citizenship classes."

The Minority VISTAs Program, which was patterned along the lines of VISTA, called into service Laredoans and area residents who were in college or had completed college studies. Manuel (Chaca) Ramirez was an organizer possessed of the ability to mobilize *barrio* residents into action.

El Cuatro was the first neighborhood to organize in 1965 as the El Cuatro Neighborhood Council.

"It was quite an event the first time someone from the *barrio* made a complicated motion at an EODC board meeting to rescind another motion in the language of Robert's Rules of Order. It took the politicians by surprise and they had to brush up on the procedure themselves," he said. "The politicians revised their opinion of the VISTAs when they realized the people of the *barrios* could speak for the needs of their neighborhoods and get something done," said Díaz De Leon, who wrote the City's initial 1964 planning grant for Office of Economic Opportunity funds.

"That first grant paid the salaries of three individuals for nine months as we set about framing what would become the scope of the EODC in Laredo. I hired Mary Devine as the secretary and Mayor Martin appointed Blas Martinez," he said. Mayor Pepe Martin served as the first president of the EODC board.

In the first component of EODC funding, War on Poverty funds established the first HeadStart program in Laredo, the Operation Mainstream work and learn apprenticeship program, and a program for remedial and tutorial education. Laredo International Fair & Exposition (LIFE) Downs was built through Operation Mainstream. It was meant to be a learning experience for carpenters, welders, plumbers, and bricklayers who apprenticed journeymen in those trades. Kenneth 0. Gilmore wrote in a 1967 *Reader's Digest* story of Laredo's "Federal Dollar Fever." A $250,000 OEC grant ear-marked for "beautification," Gilmore wrote, ended up building new stables for LIFE Downs. The grant press release stipulated that the funds would be used to build a recreational site and train jobless workers simultaneously. The jobless workers, according to Gilmore, learned to build stables of a construction much superior to their *barrio* homes.

Unusual sights began to unfold dramatically on downtown sidewalks in the late 60s as restaurant employees picketed and protested poor wages outside the Southland Cafe and Deliganis Cafeteria. Angry hand-lettered signs outside the Southland Cafe read "Huelga" (Strike) and "Starvation Wages." In the barrage of national news of the civil rights movement of the decade, there had been news of Mexican strikes of farm workers in Starr County. There was news of the

rare, politicized Catholic priest who had jumped the fence to join the strikers, and news accounts of Cesar Chavez' selfless struggle for humane treatment and better working conditions for farm workers. The word "chicano" began to surface, carrying on its sound and its meaning a polarized radicalism new to Laredo. The word heralded an outspoken Mexican-American identity in and out of the *barrio*, in and out of the crop rows. "Chicano, *chiquero*, chicanery—the word was new to me. I learned the meaning from my sons," said Díaz De Leon.

Some watched outside the Southland Cafe with curiosity, some with disdain, and many with empathy for the striking workers with their placards and black and red armbands. The strikers were angry, protesting wages of twenty-five cents an hour. They marched outside stores and restaurants, interrupting business, and asking shoppers politely at first to trade elsewhere. Many townspeople, especially those not in poverty situations and especially those encumbered by the debt of a political favor, steered clear of the protesters. Others drove around the strikers, rubbernecking or jeering. Some walked briskly to the other side of the street to avoid the taunts of the strikers. The Southland Café strike went on for more than a year, the results escalating, according to activist Juan Ramirez, when the strikers incorporated the black and red Mexican strike flag into their protest. "The flag was respected by Mexican nationals who shopped in Laredo. There were many who would not cross into a place where that flag was on display," Ramirez said.

Laredoans marched on City Hall in 1968 to push for a city-wide minimum wage and to get City Hall to stop the flow of Mexican green card commuters who worked in Laredo for absurdly low wages. According to Díaz De Leon, Minority VISTA coordinator Chaca Ramirez and San Antonio activist Willie Velásquez walked out of a Raza Unida meeting to protest the city's inaction with a sit-in at the international bridge, but a San Francisco activist-turned-mediator named German Gallegos talked them into moving their protest to a parking lot near the bridge. "Chaca marched every Monday around City Hall until there was a response from the city about a minimum wage. The city appointed Honore Ligarde to head the commission to establish a minimum wage," Díaz De Leon said, adding, "It was about jobs. People wanted to work."

Protesters who took a stand in 1968 against having to show a poll tax certificate in order to receive food commodities were tear gassed in Bruni Plaza by members of the Webb County Sheriff's Department, who did not consider whether or not children were in the group of protesters.

VISTA had come to Laredo via President Kennedy's nobly intentioned service organization and via his successor, Lyndon Johnson, as the front line on the War on Poverty. It came as no news to the poor of the *barrios* that Laredo had been declared

❖

Top, left and below: The acrid fumes of tear gas burned the eyes and skin of Laredo protesters of all ages. These pictures were snapped by Juan Ramirez in Bruni Plaza.

COURTESY OF JUAN RAMIREZ

Top, right: Officers of the Laredo Police Department tried to dissuade activists Chaca Ramirez and other protesters from a gathering outside the Laredo Civic Center.

COURTESY OF JUAN RAMIREZ

Above: Sheriff's Deputy "El Chon" held a hard line against protests that were commonplace in Laredo in the mid-sixties. He is credited with the decision to use tear gas to break up peaceful protests across the city.

COURTESY OF JUAN RAMIREZ

Below: In 1968, Minority VISTAs entered the Washington's Birthday Celebration Parade with this stakebed truck. The truck featured black and red Huelga (strike) bunting, cuernos (horns), and was filled with barrio children holding Huelga banners and placards asking for the state minimum wage in Laredo.

COURTESY OF JUAN RAMIREZ

the poorest city in the nation and Laredo had been designated the poster child for the War on Poverty. Noble purpose aside, the upshot of being a target city was the torrent of government money that would pour into local coffers and the inevitable temptation to politicize the administration of those federal funds, a finely tuned practice that has continued in Laredo well into the end of this century. The downside for the politicians was having to acknowledge the notion that the complacent poor might wish to have a voice in their own decisions.

The machine politics of Laredo are legendary, and nothing on its face is ever as simple as it appears to be. This was a machine that had the power to march the dead to the polls on election day, a machine that based job security in city, county, and school district positions on a party line affiliation, on favors owed, and service performed. It is said about those times that teachers did not apply for a job with the school district; rather they checked in at City Hall first.

There were stories.

Heroin addicts would not get their methadone doses until he or she could produce a requisite quota of poll tax receipts. A battle of wills erupted when Díaz De Leon and organizers wanted Dr. Mike Tristan, a pediatrician, on the team of doctors who would use federal Head Start funds for medical and dental examinations of children. "The local medical establishment won," recalled Díaz De Leon.

"Sargent Shriver was the head of the federal program," he said. "He came to Laredo to visit and when it was time to sit down for a meal, he sat not with the politicians that were fawning all over him, but, per his request, with those in the Azteca Center who had prepared the meal," he said.

The federally funded War on Poverty didn't bring the political machine to its knees, but it chipped away at all the old systems, managing to turn it on its deaf ear. *Barrio* activism, sparked by the VISTAS and Minority VISTAs, registered neighborhood victories in the form of water and sewer lines extended in La Ladrillera, a much needed stop light installed in El Cuatro, and street lights throughout the poorer neighborhoods.

Barrio residents became aware that it was all right to ask—no, to demand—the same utility and street provisions that were obvious amenities in better neighborhoods across town. One of the most significant VISTA contributions to Laredo politics was the registration of thousands of Laredo voters.

Clearly a thorn in the machine's side, VISTA volunteers were, according to those who didn't like them, "Yankee rabble-rousers, troublemakers, college kids, instigators." As circumstances heated up over wage strikes, one young volunteer from New York was served with arrest papers and handcuffed by a Webb County deputy. "You have to read me my rights," the VISTA worker protested. "Your rights?" The deputy did not have a copy of the Miranda with him and had to drive back to headquarters to get one before completing the arrest. There were stories of harassment of VISTA workers and the purported wiretapping of their home phones.

❖

Above: This contingent of Laredoans posed for a picture before leaving for the national Marcha de los Pobres in Washington, D.C. in May 1968.

COURTESY OF JUAN RAMIREZ

The political machine wanted VISTA gone and it began exerting pressure at state and national levels to remove them from Laredo, finding the assistance of then-Governor Preston Smith, who provided in 1967 a legal means to rid the city of VISTA by interpreting a War on Poverty guideline that allowed states to have the last word on how federal funds would be utilized.

The *barrios* remained hotbeds of dissension as old and young met on the common, dusty ground of their poverty. The political machine did in the end what it knew best to do—it absorbed into its machinations the doling out of jobs and federal funds. It politicized poverty, and by doing so allocated funds to suit itself and not the dwellers of tar paper shacks. It eventually wrested the administration of the War on Poverty funds from the Economic Opportunity Development Corporation, a panel of public officials, civic organizations, and *barrio* representatives. Under the jurisdiction of the Webb County Commissioners Court, the War on Poverty generated a bureaucracy that went into an administrative feeding frenzy on the enormous federal grants pipelined from Washington. It is said that too large a segment of the funds paid the salaries of people who were not poor. It is said, too, that there was in-fighting among the poverty agencies over federal funds. "We did the best we could," Díaz De Leon recalled. "We would choose good people for a team and then City Hall would send us *un alacrán* (a scorpion)," he said.

Inside column: Community activists were relentless in getting City Hall to establish a minimum wage and to appoint a minimum wage commissioner. Some of the placards read "Abajo Sueldos de Pobre" *(Down with Poverty Wages);* "¿Para qué prometer si no cumple, Mayor?" *(Why promise if you don't deliver, Mayor?) and "Business is going up. Why aren't minimum wages going up too?"*

COURTESY OF JUAN RAMIREZ

Ask ten Laredoans if the War on Poverty was effective, and you'll have ten diverse answers. There were benefits, to be sure, that directly affected the poor, such as Project Headstart, hot lunches for poverty-level school children, day care centers for working mothers, more available health care, and job training that improved chances for a better job. There were, too, deluxe stables built by the poor, but for which the poor had no use or desire.

The success of the War on Poverty may not be measurable at all. Nearly six million dollars in federal funds came and went like a vapor.

It should be noted that there were many dedicated War on Poverty workers who committed themselves to the letter of the law and the spirit of easing poverty, and it is likely these individuals can count successes in lives they changed through education, in the hope they inspired, in the despair they abated, and in respite and relief they brought to the daily struggle of the aged poor.

Batteries, Lots of Batteries

There is an ineluctable drama and poignancy to the content of a June 20, 1978 CBS News broadcast that zeroes in on *patronismo* in Laredo and on the winds of change that blew through City Hall in the late 70s. These were the years in

❖

Above: Laredoans traveled to El Paso in this truck to give testimony to a Cabinet Committee hearing on Mexican-American Affairs. The Laredoans testified at the invitation of Senator Ralph Yarborough.

COURTESY OF JUAN RAMIREZ

Below: Tensions rose around this protest at Bruni Plaza. Activist Roberto Valenzuela was arrested for an old traffic violation in another state.

COURTESY OF JUAN RAMIREZ

which events like a Citizens' Audit of the City Street Department, subsequent Grand Jury investigations, and new political voices portended the exit from politics of Mayor J.C. Martin, Jr., and the Old Party—events that heralded the advent of a form of city governance that would replace a century-old system.

The emotional substance of those seven or eight minutes of film in which the mayor and activist Lawrence Berry are alternately interviewed by journalist Bill Moyers present a clear build-up to the crescendo of historical events that filled the headlines and news stories of those years.

CBS REPORTS rolls film at the residence of the man who has been mayor of the City of Laredo for 24 years, a man who despite the purpose of Moyers' visit and despite the pointedness of his questions never ceases to be gracious to the visiting newsman.

Moyers sets up the story by defining a *patrón* and *patronismo*. Among other definitions, he says, a *patrón* is an individual who has the ability to manipulate thousands of docile poor people who can't speak English. In an interview in the Mayor's backyard—which a CBS film crew contrasts with the unpaved disarray of a typical *barrio* street—Moyers asks for J.C. Martin's definition of a *patrón*. Cordially, and thoughtfully, Mayor Martin tells Moyers, "You could compare *patronismo* to feudalism or something of that nature where one man or two men or a group of men had control over jobs and businesses and stores and ranches, and so on. People got to looking for those people for help or guidance when guidance was needed."

There is a glib earnestness to Martin's moments before the camera as he elaborates on the "voter education program of that date and time" and the process for the delivery of eight or nine thousand votes to state and district candidates who would best serve South Texas.

Martin tells Moyers, "A lot of people don't like to make their own political decisions, although more do now than ever before."

Moyers contrasts Martin's genteel manner with Lawrence Berry's in-your-face confrontations with the City Council at that time. There is something quite telling about what this city has been politically in the reactions of two Council members who challenge Berry "to step outside" in the moments after he asks Mayor Martin to resign. Berry tells the Mayor he should bear responsibility for the findings of a TOPS (Taxpayers Organized for Public Service) Citizens' Audit, which revealed phantom employees in the City's Street Department and outrageous expenditures for gasoline, batteries, and radiators for the department's 85 vehicles.

One council member tells Berry that his public outcry concerns are a disguise for a political campaign for Aldo Tatangelo, the politically unconnected outsider and businessman who would become Mayor in the 1978 elections.

Berry is portrayed as a persistent, hard-line advocate who sticks to the truth until the truth becomes impossible to ignore. Fifteen thousand gallons of gasoline were used by the City's Street Department every month. A bank vice-president was but one of 50 or 75 phantom employees of the Street Department; 950 car batteries were purchased over 15 months for the Street Department's 85 vehicles; $40,000 had been spent for radiator repairs. An estimate of fraudulent practices in the Street Department added up in the Citizens' Audit to about $1.5 million.

Moyers asks the Mayor how it was that such outrageous irregularities could escape him, a man whose political antennae were so finely tuned. When Martin answers, he speaks of himself sometimes in the third person: "The city grew out from under us. The duties and activities and so on of the mayor did not give the Mayor the time he should have to supervise and oversee these departments as rigidly and diligently as he should have. One of the reasons this happened is that some of us had been in office too long."

Berry appears sure and relentless with the findings of his pencil audit. He was a virtuoso rabble-rouser who could shift his focus from the fraud in the Street Department to redistricting and hammering the City for the cascades of raw sewage that flowed directly into the Rio Grande.

At the behest of District Attorney Charles Borchers, the Texas Rangers began an investigation into the Street Department's expenditures. State and federal grand juries indicted 24 Laredoans and the head of City's Street Department José (Pepe) Rodriguez.

When Moyers asks the Mayor, "Do you think the people of Laredo are ready for all this democracy?," the Mayor says, "I can't answer that. We haven't been through it in so long." It's a strange question that elicits a strange answer.

"You haven't had much democracy," Moyers interjects.

"No, we haven't had much democracy, but we're having it this year," Martin answers, a hint of wryness in his voice.

❖

In 1978 the power passed from Laredo Mayor J.C. Martin, Jr., to a Rhode Island transplant named Aldo Tatangelo, but only after an investigation that followed an open records request by activist Lawrence Berry. In the aftermath of Berry's baring of public documents, it was revealed that the City of Laredo had phantom employees drawing real paychecks and that its Street Department had purchased 950 auto batteries over 15 months for its 85 vehicles. Twenty-four Laredoans were indicted in an investigation initiated by Webb District Attorney Charles Borchers. Martin plead guilty in 1978 to one count of mail fraud for the use of the U.S. mails to pay for $250 worth of paint used on his ranch.

WEBB COUNTY HERITAGE FOUNDATIONX

Though the Berry that Moyers elicits is not especially likable, it is impossible to ignore the havoc he wreaked in the old political system and the changes he fomented. Moyers calls Berry "a sage brush Don Quixote" and says, "He has brought down the Mayor, now he intends to bring down a system." Berry tells Moyers, "I'm still alive because everything I did was very public." He adds, "We don't need to bulldoze the town, we need to change it."

The rest of the story is the history recorded in the headlines of 1978. Mayor Martin did not run for re-election. Aldo Tatangelo was elected Mayor in the April 1 elections. Mayor Martin was indicted on May 8, 1978 on one count of mail fraud that alleged that he had used the U.S. Mails to send a City of Laredo money order for the purchase of $250 in paint used at his ranch, a charge to which he pleaded guilty.

There's something else. Throughout this televised story, all along the sidelines, as though they are themselves actually an eerie sidebar to the story—and history would prove them to be—are individuals, younger looking then as the camera catches them at a poolside party, at a gala, and at the Hamilton Hotel's Snake Pit coffee shop, who were faithful to that old system and who themselves would make lifetimes of perpetuating the Old Party as it regrouped in the workings of the Laredo Independent School District and in Webb County governance.

San Bernardo Avenue in the 1950s and 60s was a beautiful artery of commerce graced by prettily landscaped tourist courts and restaurants.

COURTESY OF ROBERTO PEÑA

Some Laredo Street Stories

Town at Night

Dusk was the hour at which date palms stood like cut-out sentries against the evanescent orange band of sunset at the horizon. It was the hour at which day folded itself into night, the hour in which the skies were filled with the movement and the shrieks of day birds settling in for the night and those of nocturnals making ready for flight.

Laredo at night was like a favorite film on an endless reel. Some evenings after supper an errand might take us across town from the Heights to the downtown business district. Driving from the Heights to Zacate Creek on the Guadalupe or Market Street bridges, we entered El Azteca neighborhood. Zacate Creek with its grassy reeds and cattails divided new Laredo geographically from the old. The streets of El Azteca narrowed at the bridge, setting some of the old houses at curbside without so much as a sidewalk to distance them from the street. As passengers along the pavement we caught glimpses of the interiors of homes and lives. Some of the houses were wood board-and-batten and others were built of sandy yellow Laredo brick.

The sights on our drive changed fast as film frames as we moved toward downtown, driving past homes with their accompanying fragrances of suppers, gardenias and jasmine, and the moist earth smell of a watered-down side street. It was there at curbside, the world moving at 20 miles per hour from the Fluid Drive Plymouth or the Chevy truck with its wrap around windows that I framed the lingering images of my town, the insides of homes illuminated by the dim light of a single strand bulb to show linoleum floors, framed photos of loved ones on dark wooden furniture, kitchens in which women cooked and men waited for their suppers. Some of the screen doors facing the street effected privacy with cloth flour sacks stretched on a string across the inside. We passed the mural of the Aztec Indian and the *maguey* plant at the Kita-Tos factory, the Indian Laboratory Co.

From our slow rolling vantage we heard voices and radios broadcasting *novelas*, baseball games, and "*Radio Juventud*." Where the street widened, people sat on porches in high-backed metal chairs and gliders. Children played out of the traffic.

The drive from our home to downtown could not have taken more than a few minutes, but the texture of those drives was so rich that I remember even now that leisurely drive in and out of consciousness, absorbing the exact hue of faded ochre or turquoise paint on wood, the comforting melancholy of leaning door frames, and the precise ratio of rust to paint on the ancient red gas pumps at the Iturbide Street Texaco.

The images over time have not diminished a memory of the posture of aproned *comadres* of El Azteca visiting over wooden fences and canna lilly hedges, the resonance of the voices of tired men home from work, of children playing in the perfectly cast yellow circle beneath the street lamp, a corner *palomilla* of young men in baggy khakis.

Approaching downtown we drove past closed barbershops, bakeries, *tienditas*, furniture stores, schools, offices, and the doorways of lounges like *El Trovador*, *El Conejo*, Lucky's or the Jockey Club—doorways that emanated essences of masculine gaiety, the blues and reds of neon light.

Downtown was empty except for theatregoers, book browsers at Statler's Newsstand and a few late diners at the Southland Cafe or the Hamilton Hotel. The stores were closed in a state of restful, temporary abandonment. Merchants gone home for the day had entrusted Mr. Paksuski, the whistling night watchman, to make rounds until morning, checking locks, doorways, and lights.

With our errand completed we might elect to take a different route home past the beautiful tiles and lit fountains of Bruni Plaza and along San Bernardo Avenue and the prosperous, well-kept stretch of tourist courts and restaurants.

San Bernardo moved north to south like a ribbon ablaze in neon. The pristine swimming pools of the Evelyn Courts, the Cortez, the Gladys, and the Mayan Inn gleamed like lit oases against luxuriant oleander hedges and Washingtonia *robusta* palms. American tourists who wore bolo ties and unfamiliar hat styles dined at the Cactus Gardens Cafe and the Western Grill.

There was something all at once comforting and exciting about that familiar stretch of San Bernardo. Perhaps It was the rounded edges of the art deco tourist bungalows that conjured images of puffy yellow and pink frosted cakes. Perhaps it was the animated neon of the bucking bronc and rider at the Western Grill or the Pegasus at the Mobil station, or the repetition in red neon of VACANCY-NO VACANCY along the strip.

Beyond the illumination of the street lights and neon horses, the clouds to the open west amassed in billowing moonlit thunderheads that portended rain. The evening sky above the town was an indigo canopy of weather, stars and moonbeams, a canopy of safe passage through the good night.

❖

At the corner of Matamoros and San Bernardo, the T.J. Hall Humble Station operated side-by-side with the Humble Mexico Touring Service and the Javier Peña Insurance Agency. The one-stop site, long a fixture in downtown Laredo, offered tourists enroute to Mexico an opportunity to buy fuel, get good maps of Mexico from the General Drafting Co. of New Jersey, and buy insurance for Mexican travel.

COURTESY OF ROBERTO PEÑA

DOWNTOWN

Long before endless lines of cargo-filled tractor trailers were equated with the prosperity and well being of this city, I meandered through downtown, unfettered in the aimless absorption of the business of the life of the town.

Early morning with its dewy newness was my favorite time downtown. This was the hour at which the sidewalks belonged still to the fussy, red beaked pigeons and the street sweepers.

Along the polished, gridded Salinas Avenue sidewalk in front of Great Western Finance footsteps there resounded differently than on the walk in front of the Jarvis Plaza bandstand or the glass bricks embedded in the concrete in front of El Sol del Oriente or the Hamilton Hotel.

Oblivious to the architecture—a splendid smattering of Classic Revival (the Post Office and the old Laredo National Bank building), Art Deco (the Hamilton Hotel), Neo-Gothic (San Agustín Cathedral) and Art Moderne (the Plaza Theatre, the Farragut Store)—was found complicit solace in the familiarity of porticos, Ionic columns, fluted limestone, clerestory windows, Spanish tiles and archways.

These structural details were as much a part of the downtown vista as were the shopkeepers and clerks. This was a vista shared, too, with street vendors of fruit and ice cream, *limosneras* (the beggarwomen) and the *cartoneros* (the cardboard collectors) on their custom-made three and four wheeled carts. The street scene was punctuated at intervals with corner cops in light blue uniforms and white caps. One whistled operatic arias and another was round and portly, called by his nick-name *El Manzano*, the Apple.

One moved through wafts of curbside debris, fresh baked pastries, and smells particular to certain stores. Each doorway exhaled its own billow of fragrance and purpose, Frontier Western Wear,

Above: The Alfredo Santos grocery store at the corner of Santa Maria and Sanchez streets was a Laredo landmark for decades.

WEBB COUNTY HERITAGE FOUNDATION

Below: The Plaza Theater, built by H.B. Zachry in 1947, has been purchased by the City of Laredo, and will be restored to its former glory

WEBB COUNTY HERITAGE FOUNDATION

Sam Sullivan Shoes, and the Central Shoe Shop smelled like leather and shoe polish. Statler's Newsstand breathed Havanas and newsprint. Galo's exhaled developer and fixative. The five-and-dimes emitted essences of mothballs, popcorn, candy, and candlewax on clouds of water-cooled air. Richter's Department Store and the Bon Ton dress shop smelled like fabric and perfume. City Drug and the Walgreen with their soda fountains smelled like medicine, cologne, toast, and ice cream, depending on where you stood. The bank smelled like air-conditioned cash.

There was a checklist of familiar faces walking along the sidewalks or through stores that had doors on two streets—Mr. Levy at the G&S Office Supply, Mr. Addison at Laredo Paint and Paper, Cleo Rangel at Sam Sullivan Shoes, Santitos at Richter's, and La Morenita at the perfume counter of City Drug.

Life before styrofoam cups found old men in Jarvis Plaza playing dominoes and sipping coffee from thick paper cups with pop-out handles. Across from the Plaza, the red bricked Mercy Hospital and Jackson Funeral Home bracketed the life-to-death range of human experience. The palms and the citrus trees of Jarvis Plaza were home to pigeons, doves, squirrels, and many of the old, bearded drifters who slept in the Bender Hotel down the street.

The Kress building with its basement coffee shop, wooden floors, and Italian verdi marble footing held a special allure. Its peaked red tiled roof, yellow-orange stucco and an American eagle atop the flagpole worked like a magnet to pull pedestrians across the street and into the store for the browsing and perusing of items, such as costume jewelry, nail polish and lipstick, hair nets, berets, pink Bobby socks, household cleansers, and dolls. Children lost time, however, in careful scrutiny of toy guns, air rifles, gold fish, hamsters and parakeets, and kites.

Leaving the dark, steamy popcorn atmosphere of the Plaza Theatre, one was drawn like a dust mote to the sunny glare of afternoon and next door to the glitter of the merchandise in the windows of the Antonio González General Store. Where the sea foam green Deco tiles of the Plaza ended, there began the González show windows full of every household gadget imaginable—meat grinders, cutlery, enamelware, ladles and sieves. Another window showcased Camilus knives, switchblades, handguns, archery equipment, caps and hats. Yet another floor to ceiling showcase had every item affixable to a bicycle—streamers, handlebars, chains, reflectors, decals, mirrors, odometers and speedometers, fenders and chain guards. Bridal wreaths and silk flowers shared a window with hand tools, votive candles and oils and ointments for good luck.

Peso devaluations and the closing of Laredo Air Force Base, coupled with the move of several businesses from downtown to Mall del Norte, transformed downtown Laredo into a shadow of its prosperous 50s and 60s self. Much of the Deco charm, fluted limestone, and colored tiles have been veneered with tasteless, nondescript modernity. The Kress building, however, remains untouched, its outrageous architectural integrity intact.

At the Movies

In 1957 a dollar bought a movie ticket, popcorn, candy, and a drink. Two dollars got you the works, which included movie fare and a post-movie grilled cheese and shake at the City Drug lunch counter next door. Movies were our greatest childhood treats, except perhaps for a chance weekend in San Antonio to see the Icescapades or Roy Rogers at the San Antonio Livestock Exposition.

Movie outings were what you did with your friends on Saturdays or with your parents during the week if you had no homework. Movies were tendered as rewards for good schoolwork or make-ups for painful trips to the dentist or something as horrific as stitches or a broken wrist

There were three theatres downtown. The blue and yellow-tiled Tivoli on Flores Street across from City Hall was once called The Strand and had seen better days. It seemed like a tired place, worn at the edges and a little sticky.

The dark, cool cavern of the Royal Theatre on Hidalgo is where Saturday afternoons were spent. The Royal had also seen a more prosperous time as an outstanding opera house, but now featured for the most part movies from Mexico. The lapsed glory of the Royal was still pronounced in the ornate plastered ceilings and the pillars of the building.

Later, it was the newer Plaza Theatre that was most frequented. The Plaza faced City Hall on the Hidalgo Street side and was located between City Drug and the Gonzalez mercantile.

Built in 1947 by the H.B. Zachry Company, the Plaza's oak, tile, patterned carpeting and murals lent movie outings a hint of elegance, as did the ushers in bow ties and short blue jackets with brass buttons.

The Plaza's designers had pleased themselves repeating a lighthearted Art Deco motif throughout the structure that was façaded with sea foam green tiles and an exaggerated rounded concrete sweep around the marquee and neon towers. Large oak doors with port hole windows led into the theatre past the recessed glassed-in ticket box. A rounded stairway with a wide, hollow aluminum railing led to the balcony.

Massive wine colored drapes that were drawn before each performance fell across the Plaza's wooden stage. The walls inside the theatre were painted in a beautiful repetition of animal and jungle foliage stylized in a Fantasia-like theme.

Soft lighting emanated from thin, rounded metal wall sconces. The 1,700 seats had once been covered with plush burgundy fabric. A black light clock over the exit door kept you aware of the bus schedule back home.

Afternoon features began with "News in Brief," a black and white Universal news reel narrated by Ed Herlihy. Herlihy's voice lent a gravity to any clip, whether of strife in the Congo or those of cheesecake beauty pageants.

The Plaza brought first run movies to town—everything from *Three Coins in the Fountain* to *Dial M for Murder*. Theatres in the 50's were testing grounds for new visual and audio enhancing techniques. *The Robe*, released in 1953, was the first film in Cinemascope. Others were filmed in Cinerama or Vistavision or Surroundsound, which gave the viewer the sensation of being perilously close to menacing rivers or dangerous bluffs.

❖

Frontier Western Wear was one of downtown Laredo's anchor businesses. The store featured a basement and exhaled from its doors the fragrance of leather.

COURTESY OF MARÍA EUGENIA GUERRA

Three-D was the latest thing in moviedom. Following the re--release of *Gone with the Wind* in color, there followed a rash of movies with intermissions—*El Cid*, *Ben Hur*, *The King and I*.

The movies entertained us (*Calamity Jane*), exposed our prejudices (*Gentlemen's Agreement*, *To Kill A Mockingbird*), revealed our weaknesses (*Days of Wine and Roses*), distilled and glorified our history (*The Alamo*), hackneyed love (*Pillow Talk*), portended our horrors (*On the Beach*), and riveted us to our horsehair seats with suspense (*North by Northwest*). The antidote for movie horror was, of course, a Buena Vista Looney Tune.

The movies were a dark, cool refuge from the dry summer heat. The movies were the hub upon which friendships turned.

El Gallo Bakery: A Freeze-Frame of History Suspended in Flour Dust

El Gallo Bakery on San Agustín street offered stout coffee, fresh baked breads and pastries, and the dim, though persistent sense that it was a space indifferent to the times and changes that had overcome the rest of downtown Laredo in the sixties.

Across the street from the bustling and modernized glass-fronted El Aguila Bakery, El Gallo remained a bastion of unyielding traditions. While the city flexed its will to grow and change its face with contemporary veneers over some of the most beautiful and inspired architecture in the downtown area, El Gallo clung tenaciously to the less than modern and well-preserved, time-proven methods, menus, and service ordered by its owner, Guadalupe Ornelas. Mr. Ornelas held out with his wood-fired *hornos*, until he gave in to the practicality of natural gas ovens.

Above: The decor and fixtures of El Gallo Bakery on San Agustín Street, as well as the aroma of fresh baked bread and pastries, were a magnet for those on coffee break downtown. The business was owned by Guadalupe Ornelas.

COURTESY OF GERARDO SALAZAR

Light bulbs on a single strand of wire hung from the high ceiling over the marble aggregate U-shaped service counter, the tables, and the glass pastry cases, casting as much shadow as illumination on the archaic, filigreed steel of the old National cash register.

A massive mural of a New England landscape created irony with the arid South Texas geography just beyond the two sets of tall double screen doors. Two thousand miles from Cape Cod, an El Gallo patron might sip coffee, look past the statues of Xochil and El Indio Cuathemoc on the pastry island inside the counter's U and ponder into the painting the seaworthiness of a beached white skiff.

Some of the walls of El Gallo were brick and others were tongue-in-groove *machimbre* wainscot once enameled a light baby blue. A shiny vein of gold scrolled mirrors at eye level ran along the north wall above the wainscot and below the wide painting.

Time and use had long since worn away at the definition of sharp angles and clean, straight lines from the counter, the wooden floor and the fixtures. The creaky floor planks were worn by the presence of customers at the barstools or at the pastry cases. The wooden frames of the tall screen doors and the wide metal handles that were bread advertisements bore, too, the gentle erosion of human hands.

The glass cases held artfully shaped and textured *cuernitos*, *regalitos*, *conchas*, and *semitas*. At the service counter, customers sat comfortably on swiveled cherrywood seats and rested their feet on a brass foot rail below the counters. The Wurlitzer's repertoire provided an array of versions of love ballads from Cuco Sánchez and Agustín Lara to the songs of René and René, the local duo related to proprietor Ornelas.

It was a cavern of a building, vast and high-ceilinged, with oiled wooden floors and dim lighting.

In memory, it is clear that El Gallo wasn't just a bakery; it was a monument to resistance, a functioning environment of worn, sturdy objects, that despite their advanced age and repeated use, rendered faithful performance.

Through the archaic strains of the Wurlitzer's woestruck Mexican waltz of disconsolate violin and moody tuba in three-quarter time, through the tempting, honest vapors of *pan francés* just out of the oven, El Gallo was the successful elusion of change, an uncontrived stop-action, freeze-frame of history suspended in flour dust.

El Gallo Bakery closed its doors in May of 1971 and was flattened along with other buildings on the 600 block of San Agustín to become a parking lot.

A Corner Grocery

Chole and Don Enrique owned the corner grocery at the end of the block on Laredo Street. The store was the front room of their home which was veneered with 30s and 40s license plates nailed end on end.

The front of the store offered the shade of a tin-roofed porch which wrapped around the building. A curlicued wire fence cut off the store porch from the private porch where Chole and Don Enrique kept lawn chairs for evening chats. Chole entered the store from the darkened rooms of her home, leaving the drama of Mexican radio *novelas* that hung suspensefully

Below: Looking eastward from the Royal Opera House on Hidalgo Street, it was possible to appreciate the dynamism of the architecture of old downtown.

WEBB COUNTY HERITAGE FOUNDATION

in the atmosphere. An unexpected blast of organ and violin music signaled intense plot developments which likely heightened and colored the choices we made there.

The handles on the screen doors to the *tiendita* were metal Holsum bread loaves. A Nehi thermometer often hovered above 100 degrees in the shade of the porch. All the goods in the store were either on shelves behind the counter, in the RC Cola cooler, or in the glass cases for *pan dulce* and packaged candy and gum.

Though Chole's inventory stuck to the basics like sliced bread, Laredo Creamery Milk, eggs and some canned goods and soaps, her candy and soda water selections ran to the exotic. Besides Coca Cola, RC, and Nehi, Chole sold cold Grapette, Delaware Punch, Dr. Pepper, and Buck Brand sodas.

Chole sold Chum Gum, Fleer Double Bubble, and Bazooka. Chum Gum—which came not in flavors, but in colors, (blue or red—three sticks for a penny) was short on flavor and long on the chew, made perhaps of true chicle latex.

More than four decades have transpired since the last purchase at Don Enrique's. Still, though, One remembers the golden shafts of light that broke the fine dust that filled the store when a car drove down the unpaved expanse of Laredo Street, and still, the smell of anise seed of *semitas* and hear the rattle of small change finding its way in and out of the cash drawer under Chole's counter.

After all this time there is memory of an inexplicable pleasure to sitting on the smooth concrete edge of the store's porch drinking an icy three-cent soda, "smoking" a candy cigarette with my cousin Alfonso, or slurping the colored syrup out of the little wax soda bottles that came in a three-pack. The little wax bottles would melt, the Chum Gum stiffen and lose its flavor, but always the satisfaction of the visit to Don Enrique's lingered until the next time.

The Buckboard

Before the dusty grays and blues of evening fell on Laredo Street, the old man in the donkey-pulled buckboard passed in front of our house. You heard him before you saw him. There was the muted crunch of his thin-aired tires on gravel, and the tiny pings, creaks, and groans of the harnesses and springs of the wagon box. The clatter of pails, tools, and cargo added to the din. There was, too, the clopping of the *burro's* small hooves on the unpaved street.

The driver, a bearded junk peddler, sat on a bench. In good weather he sat straight, acknowledging people with a nod. In cold weather, braced against the wind and wearing a dark woolen overcoat, he sat hunched over the reins, hardly moving except to be sure he cleared the traffic on Cedar Avenue. In winter when the nightfall began early, he hung two lit kerosene lanterns from the roof support at the rear of the wagon.

It was not uncommon throughout the 1960s and early 70s to see horse or burro pulled carts moving along some of the streets of Laredo.

LAREDO PUBLIC LIBRARY

The cart was a light green color, painted so long ago that the finish on old wood looked more like a stain.

There was something pleasing, eerie, and familiar about the sight and sounds the peddler brought to the evening—the wagon jiggling and creaking, his load banging and the slow cadence of tired hooves.

Donkey speed with a load is slow, and his movement out of our sight and earshot was a long, delicious passage illuminated by the swaying yellow cast of his lantern light.

None of us—not my sister or my brother or my cousins—ever said we were waiting for the donkey wagon to pass, but the minutes before dusk found one or all of us on my grandmother's porch awaiting the ritual of his passage.

I don't know precisely what, other than closure for the day, that buckboard on our street signified. Perhaps it was closure for what was archaic but still useful in our lives. Perhaps the peddler and his buckboard were a spectral reminder of a late hour. We were silent, practically reverent, at the very moment at which he moved before us, and we went quickly, into our homes after he left our sight.

It did not seem possible that the donkey or the man or the cart had seen better times.

SHARING THE HERITAGE

historic profiles of businesses and organizations that have contributed to the development and economic base of Laredo

SPECIAL THANKS TO

Jamco International, Inc.

Webb County Heritage Foundation

MAJOR PERFORMANCES No. 6 — FEBRUARY 21-22, 1930.
Season 1929-1930

Little Theatre of Laredo

GORDON L. SMEDLEY, President

In Conjunction with

Washington's Birthday Celebration Association, Inc.

CHARLES DEUTZ, President

PRESENTS

"Her Song"

AND SPANISH VERBENA

IN 3 ACTS

By Special Arrangement with the

JOHN B. ROGERS PRODUCING CO. FOSTORIA, OHIO

Under Direction William E. Morgan, General Director.

Music Director — Mrs. Travis Bruce Bunn

Dance Director — Mrs. Edith Clark Lowry

Curtain 8:30 Sharp

OFFICERS

GORDON L. SMEDLEY, PRESIDENT.
FRANK LATTIG, IMMEDIATE PAST PRESIDENT.
HAL L. BRENNAN, VICE-PRESIDENT
M. H. MORGAN, TREASURER.
MRS. I. GOODMAN, CORRESPONDING SEC'Y.
MISS CORINNE DALLMER, RECORDING SEC'Y.
ED. S. RUSSELL, AUDITOR.
WILLIAM. E. MORGAN, PLAY DIRECTOR.

DIRECTORS

MISS CORINNE DALLMER
MRS. I. GOODMAN
MRS. A. C. HAMILTON
FRANK LATTIG
MATIAS DE LLANO
M. H. MORGAN
CHAS. E. READ
ED. S. RUSSELL
GORDON L. SMEDLEY
CLIFTON E. WOLCOTT

THIS PROGRAM
Furnished thru the courtesy of
THE CENTRAL POWER AND LIGHT COMPANY
Who together with all its employees heartily endorse the Little Theatre movement as well as all other moves tending to further the progress and advancement of the community which it serves.

CANTRELL & CO. 6012

Growing out of the Laredo Historical Society founded in 1955, the Webb County Heritage Foundation was chartered in 1980 and seeks to promote an awareness and appreciation of the goals of historic preservation, heritage education, and heritage tourism. In this role, the WCHF promotes preservation and rehabilitation of historic architecture, ranching heritage, and folklore and traditions of the border region. It has been instrumental in the designation of local historic districts and participates in the process of protecting the integrity of these and other areas through its work on the City of Laredo's Historic District Landmark Board. The WCHF conducts tours of historic downtown Laredo, archives historic documents, maps, and photographs, records oral histories, presents exhibitions, and operates the Republic of the Rio Grande Museum in one of Laredo's oldest structures located on San Agustin Plaza.

The Heritage Foundation celebrated twenty years of existence in the year 2000. The 160th anniversary of the declaration of the Republic of the Rio Grande was also celebrated in 2000 and was marked by the first "inauguration of the President of the Republic of the Rio Grande," an event which will become an annual opportunity to promote and encourage the development of Laredo's heritage tourism.

In 1999, the Foundation donated $20,000 to the City of Laredo as part of a matching grant to fund the rehabilitation of the historic Benavides-Herrera home at 802 Grant Street as a visitors' center.

As part of its mission of historic preservation and downtown development, the San Agustin bench replacement project represents $50,000 of private investment for beautification of a public park. Another $30,000 is expected to be raised by project completion in 2000.

The Republic of the Rio Grande Museum hosts guided tours for school-age children and adults year-round and makes presentations to schools, detention facilities, civic groups, and travel writers on a regular basis. The Webb County Heritage Foundation also provides numerous free publications in English and Spanish on subjects related to border history, heritage, landmarks, and folklore.

The Webb County Heritage Foundation office is located in the old Mercado building at 500 Flores Avenue. Office hours are Monday through Friday, 8:30 a.m. to 5 p.m.

The Republic of the Rio Grande Museum is located at 1005 Zaragoza Street. Museum hours are Tuesday through Saturday from 9:00 a.m. to 4 p.m. and Sunday 1 p.m. to 4 p.m. The museum is closed on Mondays.

❖

The Webb County Heritage Foundation archives historic documents, maps, and photographs.

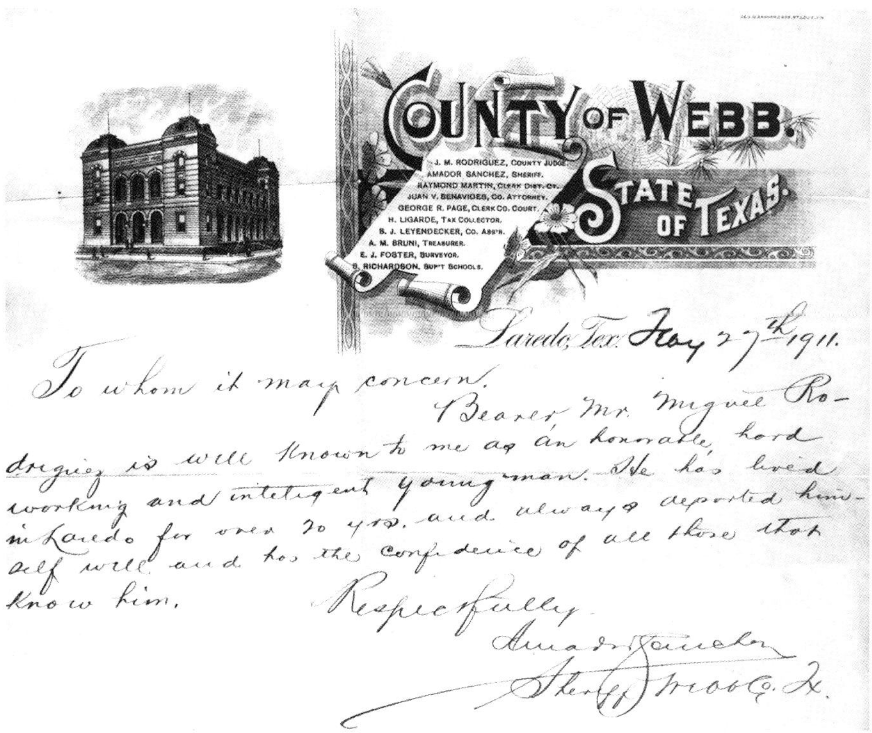

COUNTY OF WEBB.
STATE OF TEXAS.

J. M. RODRIGUEZ, COUNTY JUDGE.
AMADOR SANCHEZ, SHERIFF.
RAYMOND MARTIN, CLERK DIST. CT.
JUAN V. BENAVIDES, CO. ATTORNEY.
GEORGE R. PAGE, CLERK CO. COURT.
H. LIGARDE, TAX COLLECTOR.
B. J. LEYENDECKER, CO. ASS'R.
A. M. BRUNI, TREASURER.
E. J. FOSTER, SURVEYOR.
B. RICHARDSON, SUP'T SCHOOLS.

Laredo, Tex. May 27th 1911.

To whom it may concern.

Bearer, Mr. Miguel Rodriguez is well known to me as an honorable, hard working and inteligent young man. He has lived in Laredo for over 20 yrs. and always deported himself well and has the confidence of all those that know him.

Respectfully,

Amador Sanchez
Sheriff Webb Co. Tx.

International Bank of Commerce

Top: The late A. R. Sanchez, Sr., and Dennis E. Nixon, center, perform ribbon-cutting honors for the opening of IBC's magnificent Lago del Rio. Flanking them are (from left) Glen Jackson, Commerce Bank President Ignacio Urrabazo, and the late Father Charles McNaboe.

Below: Senior Executive Vice President Imelda Navarro and Eliza Gonzalez visit with Board member Richard Haynes at a Shareholder's Meeting.

International Bank of Commerce is committed to providing superior financial services to its customers and strong economic development opportunities to the communities it serves. This young and dynamic bank was founded in 1966 by Antonio R. Sanchez, Sr., to meet the needs of small businesses. Sanchez was a role model, a facilitator, and an economic developer who invested in people—an investment philosophy which saw IBC grow from one location to its current stature as the flagship of International Bancshares Corporation, a minority-owned holding company with over ninety financial institutions and related interests in South Texas and the Gulf Coast region.

As the largest bank headquartered on the U.S.-Mexico border, IBC is uniquely positioned to deliver on its commitment to "do more" in promoting the economic and social development of the region.

For more than a quarter of a century, IBC's international officers have developed strong, long-term relationships with top business and government officials throughout South Texas and Mexico. IBC's bilingual, multicultural banking professionals have made IBC a respected leader, particularly along the Texas-Mexico border, in international trade and finance because of their financial expertise and cultural understanding of the uniqueness of banking in border markets.

Since it's inception, IBC has reported solid financial performances each year. It has never experienced a down year in its thirty-two-year history. Its assets have increased from less than $1 million in 1966 to over $5 billion in 2000—an increase of almost 4,000 percent! This tremendous growth has made IBC the largest and best performing minority-owned bank in the nation.

Recently, the SNL Securities ranked IBC third in a five-year national performance survey of the 100 largest publicly traded banks in the United States. In addition, IBC ranked seventeenth in the country for its 1998 financial performance. IBC was the only Texas-based bank listed in the top twenty in either ranking. IBC is listed on the NASDAQ National Market and traded under the symbol IBOC.

Keeping pace with the remarkable growth is IBC's diverse range of financial products and services, meeting the needs of individuals as well as a wide spectrum of businesses—from small community-based enterprises to large multinational companies operating around the world. New products and services are developed on an ongoing basis to meet new and changing demands.

The bank's philosophy and leadership are founded in their commitment to maintain strong hometown management teams. As a result, banking professionals bring not only extensive knowledge and experience to customers, but also a unique understanding of their respective communities. This grass-roots level of involvement assures IBC's leadership is responding to and anticipating the continuously evolving needs of their customers.

IBC's explosive growth and strong financial position began under the dynamic leadership of Dennis E. Nixon, CEO and president of the flagship bank and chairman of the board for the multi-bank holding company.

Nixon became the third president of IBC in 1975. The phenomenal success of the bank and its faultless record of consecutive years of growth and profitability are directly attributable to his vision and corporate goals, his conservative credit philosophy, his aggressive management style, and the team that surrounds him.

Excellence in financial performance and service are fundamental commitments of IBC to its customers. The bank's slogan "We do more—

Above: The young staff of Laredo's newest IBC banquito location in North Laredo's Plantation area was on hand for the grand opening ceremony.

Left: In 1996, the International Bank of Commerce donated $100,000 to Friends of the Library for the purchase of books for Laredo's new public library.

Hacemos Más" reflects not only its management philosophy, but also its way of doing business and supporting the community.

Doing more means supporting, both financially and with manpower, many of the non-profit and civic groups in the communities IBC serves. In Laredo, IBC has long been a Pacesetter for United Way as the corporation matches dollar-for-dollar its employee's pledges. In 1998, IBC and its employees donated more than $110,000. IBC has also been a regular supporter of Laredo's Washington's Birthday Celebration, Bethany House, Communities in Schools, Junior Achievement, Friends of the Library, Boys and Girls Clubs, and the Boy Scouts.

One of the centerpieces of IBC's giving is the beautiful Lago del Rio, an expansive park in northwest Laredo overlooking the Rio Grande. IBC allows a multitude of organizations to host events and fundraisers at their exotic park—Laredo UT-Exes, API, Border Patrol Student of the Month, Princess Pocahontas, St. Augustine Alumni Association, and KLRN are just some of the groups who have benefited from IBC's generosity. IBC also uses the grounds to host their own events honoring Laredo's top students and recipients of the A. R. Sanchez, Sr. Memorial Scholarship and Dennis E. Nixon Scholarship. Additionally, IBC honors its own employees for their unselfish and tireless service to community.

The bank's Employee Advisory Board volunteers thousands of hours each year to events ranging from Jalapeño Festival and LIFE Downs, to MDA's Telethon and March of Dimes Walk-A-Thon, to church and school *jamaica's*. In 1999, the Laredo EAB volunteers drummed up more than 8,000 hours! IBC officers serve in leadership roles in many of the same organizations IBC supports.

IBC looks forward to continued growth and success for the bank and its clients in 2000 and beyond. Through market research and personalized attention to individuals, businesses, and communities, IBC continues to develop new and enhanced products and financial services to keep pace with the needs of their customers and their communities.

Simply stated, IBC's future, like its past and present, is built upon its unwavering commitment to "do more" for their customers and their communities.

Top: IBC proudly sponsors many events honoring Laredo's youth, this one in cooperation with the U.S. Border Patrol Students-of-the-Month.

Right: IBC matches its employee's contributions to the United Way of Laredo. In 1998, the bank and its Laredo staff contributed over $88,000.

ANTONIO R. SANCHEZ, SR.

Loving two countries and embracing two cultures, the late Antonio R. Sanchez, Sr., helped to fulfill his dream of expanded progress in South Texas as one of the founders of the International Bank of Commerce and Chairman of the Board from 1966 to 1993. Sanchez had a personal commitment to create economic and educational opportunities for the citizens of this border region.

As a descendant of Don Tomas Sanchez, the founder of Laredo, Antonio Sanchez built upon the legends of his forebearers. The family, once one of the wealthiest in the area, lost the majority of their wealth and land in the Mexican Revolution of 1910. He was born into poverty and was forced to quit school at an early age to help support his family. Volunteer Air Force service in World War II allowed him to envision for Laredo a future that included the achievement of the American dream for border residents. Ambition enabled him to gamble on the future. He knew that with hard work, perseverance, and opportunity, success would come. One of his many enterprises in his middle years was service as a lease broker for oil companies. He began to purchase mineral rights for himself in partnership with geologist Brian O'Brien. The pair began exploring for oil and natural gas. Their first drilling hit the largest oil and natural gas field in the continental United States.

Now that he had the resources, Sanchez could realize his vision for change in Laredo and South Texas through economic development. With IBC as a conduit, he was able to create an environment for success. His capital was the people of the area, himself and his talents.

He created jobs. He created opportunity. He fought for better educational opportunities for South Texas. He believed that the American dream was within the grasp of everyone, including border residents, and he made those people believe it, too. Antonio R. Sanchez, Sr., was a success story. His success and heroic efforts for South Texas fueled an economic boom that is unprecedented. His legacy is dynamic.

Left: A. R. Sanchez, Sr.

Below: Sanchez and Dennis E. Nixon in front of the vault at IBC's Laredo headquarters.

COMMERCE BANK

Commerce Bank connects its clients to a financial organization that represents billions of dollars in assets, lending leadership, and international ties that reach across borders with strength and experience while maintaining friendly, personal, first-name service.

Located in the heart of a mixed commercial and residential Laredo community, Commerce Bank has grown steadily by putting together the best of both big and small banking and combining its neighborhood partnerships with local, regional, and international business resources.

A separately-chartered member of the $5 billion International Bancshares Corporation, the fifth largest Hispanic-owned business in the U.S., Commerce Bank shares a long tradition of nurturing border business and international trade with a variety of services, including letters of credit, foreign currency exchange and wire transfers. Commerce Bank has grown from $15 million in 1983 to over $215 million in 1999.

Under the leadership of President Ignacio Urrabazo, Jr., Commerce Bank was an active proponent of the North American Free Trade Agreement and influential in its passage. Commerce Bank's international team of bilingual, bicultural banking professionals maintains strong personal and business relationships with individuals and civic, business, and government leaders in Mexico. The recent post-NAFTA international business expansion and its diversified needs have attracted a growing number of transportation and warehousing customers to the capabilities and experience of Commerce Bank.

Customers benefit from Commerce Bank's membership in the IBC family, the largest financial organization headquartered on the U.S./Mexico border. Commerce Bank and numerous IBC branches offer the advantage of proximity to Mexico-related trade with locations from Laredo to Brownsville and extending to Houston, San Antonio, and the Gulf Coast.

Well known for its informed, local loan decisions, Commerce Bank's lending program also is enhanced through its status as a Small Business Administration Certified Lender.

Located at the intersection of Bartlett and Saunders, in the medical center area, Commerce Bank completed a major renovation of facilities in the fall of 1998 to better serve its clientele.

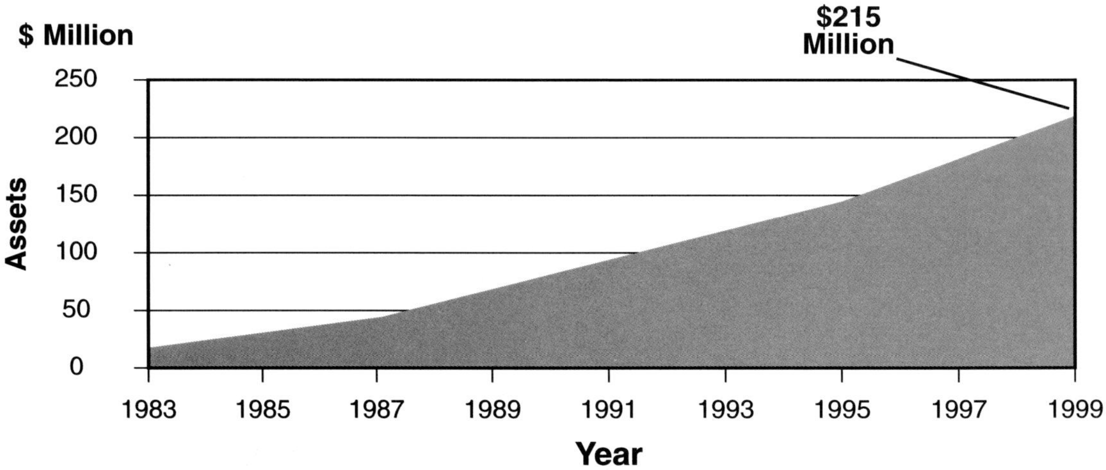

✧

Top: Ignacio Urrabazo, president, Commerce Bank.

Right: Commerce Bank's asset growth between 1983 and 1999.

Texas A&M International University

In 1968, Laredo physicians, Leonides and Joaquin Cigarroa, led a delegation to Austin asking the Coordinating Board for Higher Education to include third and fourth year classes at Laredo Junior College. They emphasized the traditional neglect of higher education on the border, as well as the discrimination of Hispanics that had plagued the state since 1836. State Representative Honore Ligarde sponsored a bill creating the upper-level institution.

In August 1969, Billy F. Cowart began work from a study carrel in the Yeary Library on the Laredo Junior College campus to create a Laredo branch studies center of Texas A&I University at Kingsville. Cowart served as president for 15 years.

Classroom and office space was leased from LJC. Degrees offered included bachelors of science in secondary education, elementary education and bachelor of business administration. An innovative International Trade Institute became famed as one of the nation's leading resources on international trade and a master's program was developed.

In May 1977, Texas A&I University at Laredo became Laredo State University (LSU) and became recognized for pioneering new approaches to education.

Senator Judith Zaffirini and Leo Sayayedra, then-president of LSU, developed long-range plans that called for expanding the institution to four-year status. In 1988, discussion began with The Texas A&M University System, a merger blessed by the Legislature in 1989. In 1993, LSU became Texas A&M International University and continues to be an innovative leader in solving the educational problems of South Texas.

Radcliffe Killam donated 300 acres of former ranch land near Lake Casa Blanca in 1993 for the construction of a new campus. Phase I and II of the construction program represent an investment of over $70 million in facilities. In 1997, current president Dr. Charles Jennett announced Phase III of the University's expansion, which will add another $45 million in new facilities.

In 1999, over 3,000 students were enrolled at A&M International, a comprehensive, state-assisted university offering 51 undergraduate or graduate degrees in the liberal arts and sciences, education and business with a focus on development of an international academic agenda.

Laredo National Bank

The Laredo National Bank was founded on February 23, 1892, in a small, one-story building on Flores Street. Laredo was small, with a population of only some 12,000, with 3,000 citizens in its sister city, Nuevo Laredo, Mexico.

Founders of the bank, John King Beretta, T. C. Frost, Joseph Deutz, A. W. Wilcox, Dario Sanchez, Thomas Caden, Raymond Martin, Fred Lithgow, Joseph Armengol, Andres Bertani, Porfirio Benavides, Joseph Christen, M. A. Hirsch, Edwin Atlee, and Louis Goodman, parlayed their financial expertise and the area's potential into a thriving concern. After the first three years of operation, they applied for and were granted National Charter #5001 and were permitted to use the name The Laredo National Bank. The small, growing bank was capitalized for $100,000 with the issuance of 1,000 shares of stock.

Over 100 years later, The Laredo National Bank (LNB) has forever changed the skyline and business climate of Laredo. This dynamic bank has served under the leadership of only seven presidents: Joseph Deutz (1895-1903), John K. Beretta (1903-1923), Isaac Alexander (1923-1938), Payne Briscoe (1939-1955), Max A. Mandel (1955-1967), Ramiro Sanchez (1967-1973), and current President and Chief Executive Officer Gary G. Jacobs, who assumed leadership in 1973.

Founded before the Federal Reserve System existed, LNB has served the personal and business banking needs of Laredo's binational community with extraordinary results. The arrival of the railroads to Laredo in 1881 created explosive growth with LNB playing an important role in driving the turn-of-the-century economy. Rail transportation allowed Laredo produce growers to get their agricultural products to large markets in the northern states.

Laredo's stature as an international port increased with World War I, when trade with Mexico expanded. Oil production in northern Mexico and in the Laredo area spurred greater shipping activity.

During the depression of the 1930s, LNB served as the depository for U.S. Treasury funds for the unemployed, issuing 3,000 weekly checks. LNB's conservative business philosophy and sound banking principals spared the bank the closures seen across the nation. Presidential executive order created a bank moratorium in March 1933, permanently closing three of Laredo's five banks. LNB was the only Laredo bank not ordered to close permanently or to reorganize—a tribute to its conservative management practices and fiscal strength.

Laredo became the "Gateway to Mexico" with the 1936 completion of the Pan-American Highway to Mexico City. World

Laredo National Bank in 1958. This building is still serving LNB customers in downtown Laredo.

War II required large quantities of raw materials, plentiful in Mexico. Import and export trade through Laredo flourished, with LNB providing much of the necessary financial services. War efforts were further aided by LNB's promotion of the sale of war bonds.

LNB recognized early the importance of diversification for the border economy and sought ways to restore prosperity to south Texas and northern Mexico during periods of economic instability. LNB became a proponent of the maquiladora industry, a twin plant concept with much of the manufacturing taking place in Mexico. Jacobs and Laredo National Bancshares Chairman of the Board Carlos Hank Rhon, with their strong international experience, have led these efforts. An upsurge in economic benefit to the twin cities has resulted. Coupled with a strengthened Mexican economy, the region is experiencing greater economic expansion, diversification, and expanded opportunities.

Officers and employees of LNB take pride in their role as community leaders who encourage and enable the growth, development and economic stability of the expanded region they serve. The LNB team devotes its volunteer time, talents, and energies to various community organizations to help meet the goal of increased advantages and opportunities for Laredo's citizens. To foster and encourage community educational development, LNB has designed and implemented programs for the youth in area schools.

LNB leaders consistently promote the economic development of the two Laredos. They have lent their voice and expertise to industrial and residential development, tourist and convention facilities, increased airline services, and additional health and higher education facilities to benefit Laredo's commerce and residents. LNB has maintained close ties with governmental officials in Austin, Washington, and Mexico City and has been instrumental in maintaining Laredo's strategic commercial importance and in procuring added benefits for the area. The LNB team has a strong commitment to education and a sincere desire to provide opportunities for area youth.

The bank's history parallels the growth and development of the south Texas and northern Mexico border over the past century. The skyline of the city and LNB has changed, but the spirit that gave birth to a financial giant and generated stability and growth is still strong and alive. Over 100 years after LNB was born in this small south Texas border town, Laredo has grown to over 180,000 residents with a sister city of over 600,000. LNB has grown into one of the strongest financial institutions in the nation and has expanded its markets to include Corpus Christi, McAllen, Houston, and San Antonio.

The future of Laredo National Bancshares, Inc. will be very bright as it builds on its deep understanding of the Mexican-American

✧

The present Laredo National Bank headquarters in downtown Laredo.

market by serving this growing segment of the population throughout Texas. While maintaining focus on the commercial and private banking business that has historically been the specialty of LNB, future expansion will be driven by an effort to provide financial services to the traditionally underserved Mexican-American population. This strategy will be focused on meeting all of the financial service needs, including loans, of the Mexican-American individual consumer and small business community.

LNB is a corporation organized under the laws of Texas in 1980, with its principal place of business in Laredo. Carlos Hank Rhon became a shareholder in 1990, assuming chairmanship of the holding company in 1991.

LNB is the fourth largest independent bank in the state of Texas. It has 20 banking offices—five in Laredo, seven in San Antonio, five in Houston, two in Corpus Christi, and one in McAllen.

South Texas National Bank was acquired in 1992. Historically, STNB has provided banking services primarily to small and medium-sized businesses and to low-to-medium income households. It has branches in Laredo and Eagle Pass.

Laredo National Bank is headquartered at 700 San Bernardo Avenue, Laredo, Texas, 78040; 956-723-1151.

St. Augustine School

Lieutenant Chief Justice Tomas Sanchez decreed Catholic education in Laredo in 1783. The first school, under the supervision of the parish priest of San Augustine Church, was conducted in a one-room building constructed of willow logs chinked with mud and adobe with a thatched roof.

St. Augustine High School, founded in 1927, was Laredo's first Catholic co-educational high school. Staffed by the Sisters of Divine Providence, lay teachers and Oblates of Mary Immaculate, the school opened its doors to grades one through five. In spite of the rigors of the Great Depression, two grades were added each year.

In the early 1970s, two local Catholic high schools—St. Joseph Academy, educating young men, and Ursuline Academy, educating young women—closed. Many of the students transferred to St. Augustine. Because the downtown school facilities could not be expanded, the school was relocated to its present address, 1300 Galveston. The Ursuline campus was purchased; allowing Catholic education to include grades Kindergarten through 12.

Accredited by the Texas Catholic Conference, an accreditation agency recognized by Texas Education Agency, St. Augustine offers a college preparatory curriculum. In addition to regular religion classes, students are given the opportunity to participate in the planning and celebration of the liturgy, the Sacrament of Reconciliation, daily prayer, class retreats, and spiritual direction. Students are guided and encouraged to participate in service activities at school and in the community. A well-rounded program of competitive sports is enhanced by a strong physical education curriculum. Participation in Student Council and various clubs affords leadership opportunities.

St. Augustine celebrated its 70th anniversary in 1997, remaining the only Catholic high school in Laredo and one of two in the Diocese of Corpus Christi. It continues to operate on the premise that values and attitudes are learned at home and enhanced in the Catholic school setting. St. Augustine has been dedicated to the mission of educating and forming young Christian men and women who are alive in the word of God in service to the Church, to the community and the world.

Top: St. Augustine School, the only Catholic high school in Laredo.

Below: St. Augustine offers classes for kindergarten through the 12th grade.

Healthcare Alliance of Laredo

Members of the Board of Managers of Healthcare Alliance of Laredo include: (from left to right) Dr. David Garza, president; Dr. Gary Unzeitig; Dr. Milton Haber; Dr. Judson Somerville; Dr. Gladys Keene; Dr. Efren Moreno; Dr. Luis Benavides; and Dr. Eduardo Gomez-Vazquez, secretary-treasurer. Not pictured: Dr. Roberto Cantu-Lara, Dr. Miguel Cavazos, and Dr. Miguel Najera, circa October 1998.

In 1992, a small group of physicians in Laredo met to discuss the future healthcare needs of the city and whether any group of physicians would be able to maintain their independence and continue to give their patients a choice of service providers in a prevailing environment of managed care, government regulation, and outside influence. These physician leaders felt that a strong, but independent organization with centralized management services would not only allow them to survive as independent practitioners, but, more importantly, offer high-quality, cost effective services to their patients. Thus, Healthcare Alliance of Laredo was created.

The goals set by these physicians were to advance the art and science of medicine in Laredo; to continue to provide consistent quality of healthcare; and promote stability in a rapidly changing healthcare environment. HAL grew over the years and by 1999, counted more than 80 independent healthcare providers from the Laredo area in its membership. HAL is an independent practice association composed of primary and specialty care providers with convenient, well-equipped offices located throughout the community. HAL physicians maintain staff privileges at all local hospitals with many serving in leadership roles in those facilities.

HAL members follow the philosophy that a patient's optimal health status can best be achieved through trust and confidence in their doctor. This relationship grows best when it is free from outside interference and when the patient can communicate with the doctor and be involved in any decision affecting his own health and well being. HAL members know that a healthy community benefits everyone, not just patients. Keeping Laredoans healthy is the principal goal of the Healthcare Alliance of Laredo.

Most of HAL's members have deep roots in the Laredo area and offer their time and talents to a wide variety of civic and community services and organizations. They hold prominent positions in state and county medical societies, local school districts, colleges and universities, and civic and cultural organizations as well as healthcare organizations, frequently participating in health fairs, education programs, and screenings designed to better educate the population on healthcare matters and early recognition of certain diseases.

As the new millennium approaches, Healthcare Alliance of Laredo stands ready to meet the area's healthcare needs and knows that there will be more opportunities to serve the increasing needs of this expanding community. HAL members will continue to take advantage of those opportunities without forgetting HAL's primary goal of "patients first."

Healthcare Alliance of Laredo, 800 East Mann Road, Suite 202, Laredo, Texas 78041, (956) 724-6546.

ALLERGY/IMMUNOLOGY
Dr. Gladys C. Keene
Dr. Jane C. Unzeitig

ANESTHESIA
Dr. Ernest Aqui
Dr. Jose Gomez-Vazquez
Dr. Victor Lopez
Dr. Renan Santos

CARDIOLOGY
Dr. Octavio E. Guzman
Dr. Ralph Nimchan

CARDIO-VASCULAR SURGERY
Dr. Alfonso Chiscano
Dr. Javier J. Marcos
Dr. David Nielson

CHIROPRACTIC
Dr. Michael S. Setliff
Dr. Duane Vincent

EAR, NOSE & THROAT
Dr. Paul R. Buitron
Dr. Roger H. Keene

EMERGENCY MEDICINE
Dr. Sebastian Padron

FAMILY PRACTICE
Dr. Luis Benavides
Dr. Oscar Benavides
Dr. Elva Camero
Dr. Rene Compean
Dr. Gustavo Garcia-Ramos
Dr. David Garza
Dr. Isaias Garza
Dr. Eduardo Gomez-Vazquez
Dr. Jorge Gomez-Vazquez
Dr. Luis O. Mendoza
Dr. Francisco I. Peña
Dr. Jesus Pineda
Dr. Renan Santos
Dr. Humberto Varela
Dr. Gustavo Villarreal
Dr. Eloy Zamarron, Jr.

GASTROENTEROLOGY
Dr. Reynaldo Godines

GENERAL SURGERY
Dr. Roberto Gomez-Vazquez
Dr. Manuel Gonzalez
Dr. Robert K. Maddox
Dr. Jose E. Molina
Dr. Miguel E. Najera
Dr. Gary W. Unzeitig

HEMATOLOGY/ONCOLOGY
Dr. Eduardo Miranda

INTERNAL MEDICINE
Dr. Jose R. Garcia
Dr. Milton Haber
Dr. L.F. Mendoza, Jr.
Dr. Leo Valentin
Dr. Winder Vasquez

NEONATOLOGY
Dr. Jose L. Berlioz

NEPHROLOGY
Dr. Carlos A. Espinosa

OBSTETRICS/GYNECOLOGY
Dr. Eliud Acevedo
Dr. Enrique F. Benavides
Dr. Carlos Cruz
Dr. J. Santiago Gutierrez
Dr. Juan Montalvo
Dr. Sigifredo Perez
Dr. Antonio Salinas
Dr. Wlfrano Sanchez

OPHTHALMOLOGY
Dr. Alfredo Treviño
Dr. Luis Zaffirini

OPTOMETRY
Dr. Max I. Friedman

ORTHOPEDICS
Dr. Roberto J. Cantu-Lara
Dr. Michael Galo

ORTHOPEDIC SPINAL SURGERY
Dr. M. David Dennis

PAIN MANAGEMENT
Dr. David M. Hirsch
Dr. Victor Lopez
Dr. Judson Somerville

PATHOLOGY & LABORATORY MEDICINE
Dr. Luis Llamas
Dr. Oscar Ramos

PEDIATRICS
Dr. Avelino C. Alvarez
Dr. Hector M. Cantu
Dr. Pedro Castañeda, Jr.
Dr. Miguel A. Cavazos, Jr.
Dr. Amando Garza, III
Dr. Gladys C. Keene
Dr. Antonio Rodriquez

PEDIATRIC NEUROLOGY
Dr. Daniel Garza

PLASTIC SURGERY
Dr. Efren Moreno

PODIATRY
Dr. Daniel Bell
Dr. Curt Griffis

PSYCHIATRY
Dr. Jose G. Garcia
Dr. Homero R. Sanchez

PULMONOLOGY
Dr. L. F. Mendoza, Jr.
Dr. Winder Vasquez

RADIOLOGY
Dr. Carlos Gutierrez
Dr. Dale Vincent

RADIOTHERAPY
Dr. Manuel A. Jovel

UROLOGY
Dr. Armando Lopez

VASCULAR SURGERY
Dr. Manuel J. Gonzalez

Laredo Community College

Laredo Community College, rich in history and tradition, is situated on the grounds of historic Fort McIntosh on a scenic bend of the Rio Grande. LCC was born as Laredo Junior College in 1944 when the fort was abandoned by the U.S. Army and deeded over to Laredo Independent School District for use as a junior college as the need for post-secondary education increased after World War II.

LJC opened its doors to students in the Fall of 1947, providing educational services to area students and returning veterans seeking job skills training. Classes were originally geared toward vocational preparation in homemaking, applied arts, business education and trades. Courses leading to self-improvement were offered in the fields of art, music and literature.

✧

Illustrations depicting buildings from the Laredo Community College campus.

ARTWORK COURTESY OF JESUS A. CARRIZALES, LAREDO COMMUNITY COLLEGE.

In 1992, LJC became LCC. Today, the 200-acre campus is comprised of the fort's historic wooden and brick structures dating to the turn of the century as well as modern brick structures built primarily in the 1970s.

LCC enrolls more than 10,000 students annually and is a comprehensive community college committed to the provision of education services that meet the needs of its community, citizens and service area.

Offerings include occupational programs, transfer curricula (including an Associate of Arts degree and an Associate of Science degree), adult and continuing education, and developmental education, student development services and community services. Transfer courses are designed to satisfy the requirements of the first two years of a baccalaureate degree. Technical and occupational training leads to the Associate of Applied Science degree with coursework designed to prepare graduates for entry-level employment. Other vocational courses and certificates are tailored to meet the needs of local manufacturers and businesses.

Dr. Ramon H. Dovalina, who took office in 1995, is LCC's fifth president. He was preceded by W. J. Adkins, named the first president in 1947; Dr. Ray Laird, 1960; Dr. Domingo Arechiga, 1974; and Dr. Roger Worsley, 1985.

Fort McIntosh was originally established as Camp Crawford in 1849, near the point of an old Indian and Spanish river crossing.

Named for George W. Crawford, Secretary of War under President Zachary Taylor, it was soon renamed Fort McIntosh, for Lt. Col. James Simmons McIntosh, a hero in the Battle of Molino del Rey. Several Texas border forts established at the same time were named in honor of fallen officers of the Mexican-American War.

Today, Fort McIntosh is marked by four distinctive architectural eras: Early Fort McIntosh Period, 1849-1861; Civil to Spanish-American War Period, 1861-1898; Modern Fort McIntosh Period, 1900-1945 and Laredo Community College Period, 1946 to present. Campus street names honor fallen heroes, presidents, fort commanders, officers and soldiers.

The post was created initially to quell the raids of the Lipan Apache and Comanche Indians and the bandits who plagued the area. Abandoned during the Civil War, the Fort was reestablished during Reconstruction. Among the troops stationed here were several African-American units, including the famous Tenth Cavalry Buffalo Soldiers.

An earthen star fort was constructed by troops in the early 1850s. From it, the troops could fire on the enemy from relative safety. The remains of this fort are visible.

Col. Robert E. Lee visited the fort on two occasions, in 1856 on his way to a court-martial at Ringgold Barracks at Rio Grande City and in 1860 while giving chase to Mexican revolutionary Juan Nepomuceno Cortina.

The first official military reconnaissance flight in history took off from Fort McIntosh to Eagle Pass on March 3, 1911, gathering military information of troop movements in Mexico and marking the beginning of military aviation in the U.S. During test flights the first aerial photos in history were taken.

As many as 30,000 soldiers trained at Fort McIntosh during World War I. Many of the fort's wooden structures were built during this time. Fort McIntosh is listed in the National Register of Historic Places and is listed as a Texas Archaeological Landmark by the Texas Historical Commission.

Laredo Community College's physical location is also its mailing address: West End Washington Street, Laredo, Texas 78040; 956-722-0521.

Modern Machine Shop, Inc. and Modern Construction, Inc.

Left: Manuel B. Garcia.

Right: Ruben Garcia.

Brothers Manuel B. and Ruben Garcia founded Modern Machine Shop, Inc. in 1941 as a small repair shop behind their mother's home at the corner of Marcella and Corpus Christi Streets. In 1944, Modern Machine Shop moved to 2009 Guadalupe, increasing the shop's size and capabilities. The company performed general machine shop work and fabricated construction parts and elements for agriculture and petroleum industries.

By 1965, the growth of Laredo's inland trade had begun to place formidable demand on the company's services. Needing a facility that would permit greater volume and diversification of services, the brothers relocated their shop to the Zapata Highway. Each move saw an increase in building and company size, as well as an expansion of services.

Modern Machine's diversified operations and capabilities now include fabrication of products for worldwide use in machine work and the petroleum industry. The company fabricates forms for bridges, dams, tunnels for underground transit systems, water control tunnels, airfield structures and hydraulic compacting trash units for city sanitation pick-up. The market distribution of these products expands through the United States, Mexico, Spain, Israel, Lebanon, Hawaii, Puerto Rico, and the Philippine Islands.

A rapid expansion of the need for metal warehousing provided the impetus for expansion into another venture. Modern Construction, a division of Modern Machine Shop, Inc., was started in 1972, marking the beginning of fast-paced commercial metal warehouse construction and leading to the development of Modern Industrial Park, a hub of import and export business between the United States and Mexico. Modern Construction, formulated under the guidance of a second generation of Garcias—Manuel's sons Ruben M., Sergio M., and Hector G.—became the exclusive dealers for Southern Structures Building Systems of Lafayette, Louisiana, a prefabricated construction system. This division rapidly expanded its base of operations to include projects in Houston, San Antonio, Victoria, Zapata, Eagle Pass, Del Rio, and other Texas cities.

Modern Construction separated from its mother corporation and was chartered as a separate corporation in 1977. This division became Modern Construction, Inc. As sister corporations, they continue to work harmoniously.

Modern Construction builds schools, office buildings, churches and other customized buildings with its 100 to 110 employees. Several prominent Laredo commercial structures serve as testimony of the company's ability to sustain the hallmark of delivery of quality merchandise and efficient service. This division has also taken on remodeling work and custom structural design projects. The relationship with Modern Machine enables the company to rapidly secure specialty design fabricated steel for projects.

The dual companies have developed additional industrial parks, Tejas I, Tejas II, and Tejas III between 1980 and 1986, constructing 95 percent of existing warehouses in Laredo. These industrial parks are located between IH-35 and Mines Road, north of Laredo. Additionally, Modern Construction, Inc. started and is currently developing UNITEC Industrial Park, located approximately ten miles north of Laredo on IH-35. At the same time, Modern Machine Shop, Inc. has fabricated steel for ten HEB's located in Laredo, San Antonio, Austin, Corpus Christi, Brenham, Uvalde, and Eagle Pass.

The major elements in the successful growth of both Modern enterprises are the continuance of family guidance, solidarity within the company's brain trust and the ability to recognize and adjust to local industrial trends in an effort to service the demands of Laredo businesses.

The elements of premium merchandise and courteous and consistent customer/employee relationships are the foundation on which Manuel B. and Ruben Garcia built their business. The expansion of the metal warehouse and more recent tilt-up wall warehouse markets provided solutions for unprecedented growth to meet import/export demands in the city. Modern Construction became the trailblazer in prefabricated construction.

Ruben M. Garcia, current president of both enterprises, has lent his immeasurable personal expertise in the business world to various Laredo organizations. A widely recognized and sought after civic leader, he has assumed active roles on the Laredo Chamber of Commerce Board of Directors, Laredo Junior College Board of Trustees, Greater Laredo Development Foundation Board, South Texas Work Force Board, Private Industry Council, and Laredo International Fair and Exposition. He also served as Trustee of the Union National Bank, South Texas National Bank and currently serves as Central Power and Light Company Trustee. In the past he was active with Little League and Boy Scouts and recently became a Laredo Junior Achievement Laureate.

The third and fourth generation of Garcias are now at work in both enterprises. Modern Machine Shop and Modern Construction have roots set deep in the history of Laredo's growth and development. Through visionary leadership, professional staff and a commitment to sustaining the basic qualities on which the original company was founded in 1941, these sister companies will continue to meet the diversified needs of Laredo's machining, fabrication, construction and warehouse industries.

In 1990, both Modern Machine Shop, Inc. and Modern Construction, Inc. relocated to 2000 Blaine, three blocks south of Zapata Highway, (956) 722-4656, where both companies continue to serve Laredo with total dedication and professionalism.

Modern Construction founder Manuel B. Garcia and his sons. First row: Manuel Garcia (left) and Ruben M. Garcia. Second row: Sergio M. Garcia, Manuel Garcia, III, and Hector G. Garcia.

Sony

Sony lives on the cutting edge. Its business demands it. In 1979, Sony Magneticos de Mexico was created with 60 employees who were responsible for the assembly of parts and components to make audiocassettes. Sony operates a *maquiladora* (twin plant) in Laredo/ Nuevo Laredo, with the bulk of the labor done in its three modern plants in Nuevo Laredo, Mexico and has established a Receiving Center and National Distribution Center in Laredo.

Sony plants possess and create the latest technology available worldwide. In 1980, the corporation created the 3.5-inch micro floppy disk for computers. Since 1984, the micro disk has been adopted worldwide. Sony currently manufactures more than 50 models of audiocassettes and micro disks. Millions of its products are shipped to the most varied and distant markets.

Top: Garden in the entrance to the Data Media Plant in Nuevo Laredo, Tamaulipas, Mexico.

Below: Fountain in the entrance to the Audio and Video Consumer Plant in Nuevo Laredo, Tamaulipas, Mexico.

Sony assures that the disk it produces is the best on the market. Aside from developing it, Sony offers a disk with a guaranteed format. It utilizes embossed shutters to avoid the use of liquid inks. The disks consume small amounts of energy because its design offers little resistance to the friction inside the drives. Its plastic shells are specially treated to avoid dust and contamination inside the body of the disk. The micro disk meets market demand for a product that tolerates office and external environments and that guarantees the integrity of the disk's information.

In 1986, Sony began manufacturing components and parts required for its own assembly processes and to meet its own standards of quality, cost, and opportunity. Such a move also allowed them to increase equipment productivity and maintain the necessary capacity to produce external components. In 1997, the micro disk floppy shutter stamping process was integrated. The division began to produce parts for automobiles and televisions for Mexico, small parts and audiocassette shells for Italy and cases for data cartridges for the United States.

At the end of 1994, Sony established a refurbishing operation in Laredo/Nuevo Laredo—their Consumer Product Center. Due to the competitive nature of the consumer electronic

industry in the United States and Sony's high standards of consumer satisfaction, Sony allows wholesalers and retailers to return products for any reason. These products are received in Laredo and refurbished in Sony's Consumer Product Center Plant by skilled employees trained to meet original equipment specifications with sophisticated diagnostic equipment and new original Sony parts. These products are returned to the market through Sony outlet stores, dealers, and distributors with a warranty that they will perform as well as one just off the assembly line.

Sony's processes are constantly improving, generating opportunities to advance technologically in order to maintain competitiveness in the world market. For instance, Sony transformed the audio manual winding process to an automatic one with in-house engineering; implemented a tape editor machine; used a synthetic pressure pad in place of one made of wool; made paint substitutions in the printing machines; created a closed cabin system for machines; and installed a new inspection system. In 1998, Sony introduced the assembly of rechargeable lithium batteries. These innovations have allowed Sony to increase machinery and equipment productivity as well as reduce manufacturing costs and reach the highest standards in quality.

Personal training and development, continued innovation, creativity, constant change and fast action are daily ideas that the Sony family contributes to its growth and prestige. Sony considers its employees its most valued asset.

Laredo and Nuevo Laredo were selected for this Sony plant because they are found at the center of the American continent. The location provides all the necessary infrastructures for the company and is a strategic point of worldwide distribution through any type of transportation method required.

Sony has a close and friendly relationship with local and regional schools and universities, reflected through a permanent program of professional practices and residencies by students and teachers as well as through diverse courses and seminars. In 1990, in coordination with the Mexican government, Sony established an adult education program that has given over 200 employees the opportunity to earn junior high and high school certification.

Sony has a great image and prestige in the community due to its continuous involvement as a good corporate citizen.

✧

Above: The Consumer Products Center Facility in Nuevo Laredo, Tamaulipas, Mexico.

Below: The Logistics and Distribution Center in Laredo, Texas.

La Bota Ranch

Nestled along lazy curves of the Rio Grande lies a very special place where fertile *vegas* (river bottoms) run abruptly into the stark beauty of the desert prairie. Towering bluffs overlook the lazy river current, red-tailed hawks and red-winged blackbirds share the vast skies and deer and javalina scamper across rock ridge tops and through arroyos.

This historic setting is the La Bota Ranch; named for the boot shape the Rio Grande carves out of the land at that location. Its roots are traced to one Sunday morning in June 1767, when a visiting Spanish Royal Commission apportioned tracts of land to the original settlers of San Agustin de Laredo. La Bota was formed from *porciones* 15, 16, 17, 18, and 19 as pasture-lands for the Ortiz family.

Until recently, this family owned the Casa Ortiz, facing Laredo's town square, which sports a plaque denoting its five generation heritage. In 1937, L. R. Ortiz sold parts of this original Spanish ranch land grants to Albert Furney Muller, Sr. and was the first known sale of local land grant property. The Muller family was another family deeply rooted in Laredo, having established the Muller Dairy, one of the first dairies in the city, in the 1800s. Albert's grandmother, Ida McLaughlin Muller, ran the dairy.

A. F. Muller, Sr. was a visionary. He knew that the La Bota was a very special place. Ironically, his son, A. F. Muller, Jr., married Virginia "Cookie" Muller, niece of L. R. Ortiz, reuniting the family and the land.

La Bota is located north of Laredo, off Mines Road, which historically served as a route to the coal mines in northern Webb County. Today, Mines Road is well trafficked, leading cars and trucks to Laredo's industrial centers and across the Colombia Bridge. Soon it will bear traffic to Laredo's fourth bridge, near La Bota.

Residents of La Bota's master-planned community leave the hustle and bustle of a growing Laredo behind within seconds of driving through the unique wrought iron and stone entrance. Within the confines of their neighborhood, meticulously landscaped commons areas featuring native flora greeted them.

Panoramic views of the natural washes and undulating landscape characteristic of the desert southwest foster a sense of pride and respect for the land and the community which calls it home.

Albert Muller, Jr., developer, along with other family members, had safety foremost in his mind when planning the La Bota Ranch development. A 24-hour manned security gate assures residents continuing natural quiet and safety of privately owned streets. Enhanced traffic control gives residents a feeling of confidence in the protection available for family.

The developers of La Bota Ranch are committed to establishing an exclusive master-planned community that retains its environmental heritage while holding high standards for residences. Neighbors share common greenbelts and amenities, including a private park with a pond, swimming pool, hike and bike trails, recreation areas, children's playgrounds, tennis and basketball courts, and a community center. Great care has been taken to make this community one-of-a-kind in South Texas. Neighborhood streets end in cul-de-sacs which offer safety and privacy with minimal through traffic.

Cardinal Creek, La Bota's first neighborhood, created a viable homeowner's association, which expands to include new neighborhoods, such as Hummingbird Creek Mockingbird Terrace, Cinnamon Teal, and Mockingbird Heights.

To ensure the success of their project, the developers of La Bota Ranch have joined with community members to establish the La Bota Ranch Foundation to sponsor the community's Julia Bird Jones Muller Elementary School. The Foundation will partner with the school to set educational benchmarks for the future and ensure that resources are available to meet its needs.

La Bota Ranch is a place where history is helping to form new traditions.

La Bota Ranch is located at 307 A. F. Muller, Sr. Memorial Boulevard, Laredo, Texas 78045; 956-726-9891.

City of Laredo Office of the Mayor & Planning and Development Department

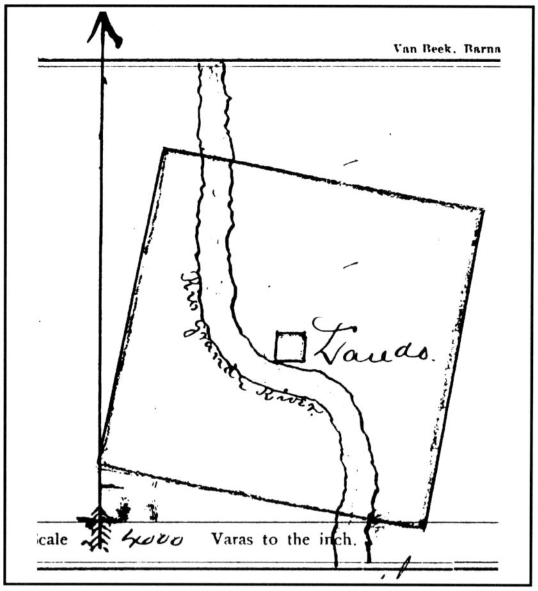

Laredo's development from a small Spanish *rancho* into one of the largest inland ports in the United States is a two-and-a-half century drama of determination to overcome the adversity of a desert environment and invent a border culture focused on the life-giving Rio Grande. A hallmark of the city's urban morphology is its street grid based on a sixteenth century Spanish settlement system imported to the New World. Today, Laredo's Latin American style settlement pattern is coupled with modern suburban growth of the twentieth century, generating a dynamic urban space shared by both the United States and Mexico.

Tomás Sánchez founded Laredo in 1755 as a family *rancho* on the northern bank of the Rio Grande. In 1767, Juan Fernando de Palacios, governor of Nuevo Santander, New Spain, officially designated Laredo as a *villa*, laid out a central plaza and issued *porciones*, or land grants to settlers. Town lots were assigned for public and private uses and six leagues of land surrounding the *villa* were designated as *ejidos*, or common pastures. Town lots measuring twenty-by-forty *varas* were laid out around the plaza.

Central to the plan was the rectangular plaza. The plaza was used to corral cattle during roundups for branding and for public gatherings, such as the *visita general*, or the reading of decrees. The plaza was an integral part of the Spanish town plan in the New World. It was the starting point for the town, the center of civic life and was the pivotal space from which the entire town's plan evolved.

Following the Civil War, Mayor Samuel Jarvis expanded this traditional Spanish plaza town plan. Knowledgeable in engineering, Jarvis surveyed the city to advance its development. In 1869, City Council adopted his new street plan, which called for the naming of streets alternately for Mexican and American war heroes.

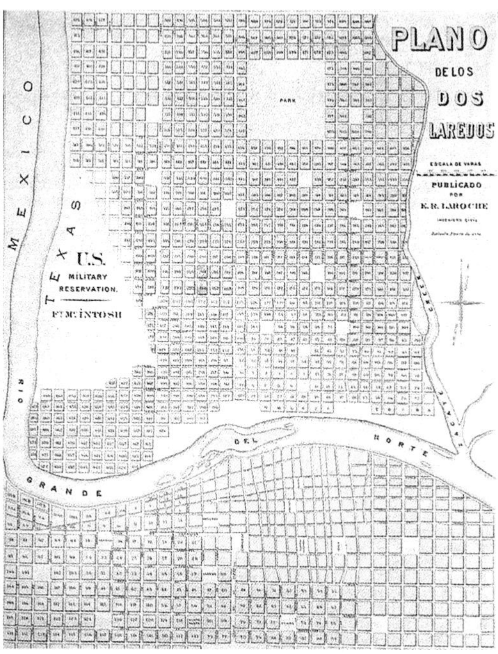

✧

Top, left: 1875 survey of original Spanish boundaries, Webb County Survey Books.

Top, right: Map of Laredo, 1757 Inspection Report, British Museum.

Right: Plano de los dos Laredos *by E. R. Laroche, 1881, Colección Tamaulipas.*

Laredo was transformed from a *villa* to a booming "gateway" city with the arrival of the railroads in 1881, becoming a major trade thoroughfare between the U.S. and Mexico. The city's population tripled from 3,521 in 1880 to 11,319 in 1890 as emigrants from Europe and all parts of the U.S. moved to Laredo seeking employment and business opportunities.

The 1890 city map shows an expanded town plan with twenty-three plazas. All of the *ejido* land was subdivided into blocks, creating the eastern and western divisions with Zacate Creek being the point of division.

The automobile spurred expansion of Laredo's residential areas. In 1921, Laredoans voted bonds to pave 104 blocks of streets. One of the first developments outside *ejido* boundaries was Calton Gardens, north of the City, platted in 1926. South Laredo neighborhoods of Montrose, Chacon, and Santo Niño developed within *ejido* lands. Sometime after 1935, San Bernardo Avenue replaced Santa Maria Avenue as the road to San Antonio. Tourist camps, restaurants, auto repair shops, and filling stations lined the avenue to accommodate the auto tourist.

With the establishment of the Laredo Air Base by the U.S. Army on 1,500 acres during World War II, the city expanded northward. To meet the demands of the post-war boom, the City created the Planning Commission charged with developing a master plan for city development in 1956. The Commission was also charged with exercising control over platting and making recommendations to the Council for a zoning plan. In 1964, the Commission's name was changed to the Planning and Zoning Commission.

To implement growth and development based on modern planning principles, the City established a Planning Department in 1979. In 1980, a Land Development Ordinance was adopted by the City Council, providing for subdivision regulations. A Zoning Ordinance was adopted in 1983. In 1991, the City's Comprehensive Plan, which was adopted in 1965, was amended. At the same time, the Major Thoroughfare Plan and the Future Land Use Plan were adopted. These plans established policies toward growth, development and the provision of public facilities and services through the 2010-planning horizon.

Today, the Planning Department is recognized for its binational planning process. The Urban Plan of Los Dos Laredos incorporates the elements of land use and transportation while defining joint planning goals which include environmental protection, development of tourism, alleviation of traffic congestion, historical and cultural preservation and facilitation of international commerce.

In its 245-year history, Laredo has undergone a metamorphosis from a small Spanish *villa* to the largest inland port in the United States. Today, the task of guiding Laredo's fast paced development, meeting transportation infrastructure demands, and revitalizing the city's historic core is lead by Elizabeth G. Flores. Flores, who made her mark in history as the city's first woman mayor in 1998, continues the city's tradition of strong leadership and individual character.

Top: Laredo's first woman mayor, Elizabeth G. Flores.

PHOTO COURTESY CALEB BOLCH, AVALON STUDIOS.

Below: A perspective map of Laredo, 1890.

Rio Grande Plaza by Howard Johnson

Looming above the riverbank, visible on any approach to the downtown Laredo area, the Rio Grande Plaza by Howard Johnson is the tall, round edifice on the Rio Grande. This resplendent towering structure recently underwent a $2 million dollar renovation.

The hostelry boasts 201 spacious rooms and three specialty suites. Forty of the 201 rooms are junior suites, fully equipped with a microwave and refrigerator. The pie-shaped rooms are larger than the average hotel room—the largest in Laredo—providing spacious accommodations for the business traveler—with fax and modem access—the traveler with a lot of baggage, families, and groups.

The current decor introduces the hotel guest to the Spanish roots of the Laredo area, done in hacienda style, with warm, large, earthy furnishings. In the lobby area, guests can even find hand-made hacienda-style Mexican furnishings for sale.

Meeting and banquet facilities are spacious, with two locations occupying 4,100-square feet. Choose a space with a panoramic view on the hotel's 15th floor or in the lower level of the hotel. The Windows on the Rio Ballroom transforms into the Castillian Tower Club for special events. The hotel offers full-service catering and banquet menus for up to 300 persons and will also coordinate with outside caterers to please clientele.

The River View restaurant on the main floor offers diners a variety of menu options to please

hungry palates from 6:30 a.m. to 11 p.m. Thirsts may be soothed with hearty libations at the adjacent River View Club from 5 p.m. to 2 a.m. with a happy hour from 5 to 8 p.m. featuring free hors d'oeuvres, music, and beverage specials. Live musical entertainment is provided on the weekend on the 15th floor or in the main level lounge.

The Rio Grande Plaza staff works hard to ensure guests enjoy their Laredo sojourn. Staff will assist tour and convention groups in planning tours, activities, and events around conferencing and will even work with Riverdrive Mall and downtown merchants to prepare individual goodie bags for conventioneers. Security cameras

and in-house security staff ensure guest safety; the hotel shuttle will transport guests to various points in the city; free parking is adjacent to the hotel; and, of course, bellmen are plentiful. Guest amenities feature courteous valet and room service, an on-premises coin laundry, non-smoking and handicap accessible accommodations. Many rooms offer a view into Mexico. On occasional weekends, vendors in the lobby offer jewelry, silver, and craft items for sale.

Future expansion by the City of Laredo to create a greenbelt around the riverfront area will place Howard Johnson's in the midst of a natural recreational area.

This round hotel on the Rio has a remarkable past. It was initially constructed in 1977 as a Hilton Hotel by Riverdrive Mall developer Vicente Garza, fulfilling a long-time dream. Garza had seen a round Holiday Inn in Austin and was fascinated by it. So, he brought the concept home to Laredo, played with the design and created the imposing structure on the Laredo skyline to capitalize on Laredo's attractiveness as a shopping destination.

Garza secured a franchise for his hotel from Baron and Eric Hilton to offer visitors to Laredo a luxurious option for overnight stays. At the time, guests from Mexico and other places would make large seasonal purchases in Laredo, often coming for an extended shopping trip. Many desired luxury accommodations. The Hilton provided this plus offered proximity to a plethora of shops in Garza's Riverdrive Mall and the downtown market center. Many visitors enjoyed the historic ambiance of the downtown area and the panoramic view from the hotel, as well as the harmonious accommodations.

At today's Rio Grande Plaza by Howard Johnson, luxurious attention is still being provided to guests, who may avail themselves of a variety of accommodations and services. Rio Grande Plaza, One South Main Avenue, Laredo, Texas, 78040; 956-722-2411.

Webb County Title & Abstract Co., Inc.

Fueled by the perceived necessity for quality real estate title services to Laredo and Webb County realtors and residents, Webb County Title and Abstract Co., Inc., was begun in 1974 as South Texas Abstract. Raquel Gonzalez, current president, was initially an investor and vice-president. She took over management of the company in 1988.

Gonzalez began her business career at the age of twelve assisting her father in his auto body and repair shop. Her skills as a businesswoman were evident early, mentored by her father.

Diversification of her interests has led her into many fields, including real estate and commercial investments. Her enterprising nature thrived on the accomplishments gained by hard work, intelligent planning and common sense. Her work in real estate in a community and county that was growing at a rapid pace led her to believe that additional abstracting services were needed for the community. Her investment in South Texas Abstract was an extension of her unerring business acumen.

When her investment in the abstract company was imperiled as the business faced failure, Gonzalez assumed the reins of control, turning the business around. Today, Webb County Title and Abstract Co., Inc. is headquartered in a modern facility on busy IH-35, with a branch office at 6414 McPherson. The company employs thirty people and is in the process of automating all operations. The company specializes in title insurance, escrow and real estate closings and is an agent for Alamo Title Insurance of Texas, United General Title, and Fidelity National Title Insurance Company.

Gonzalez has been a steady influence in Laredo's business world, ever broadening her interests and endeavors on the part of the community. She serves on the board of the Laredo Housing Authority and is an elected member of the Laredo Community College Board of Trustees, in addition to service to many of Laredo's non-profit and civic organizations.

✧

Top: Raquel Gonzalez, president of Webb County Title & Abstract Co., Inc.

Left: Webb County Title & Abstract Co., Inc. offices at 1620 Santa Ursula.

Sames Motor Company

William J. Sames came to Laredo in 1889 via Connecticut, Cuba, and Mexico. A bout with pneumonia in Mexico sent him to a drier climate and an introduction to J. O. Nicholson and his nephew, J .R. Moore. Sames and Moore became friends and partners.

In 1910, the duo began Laredo Auto Sales Company (LAS) with the purchase of three Model T's. The first cars were delivered by train, unassembled. The dealership sold the first Fords in the counties of Duval, Jim Hogg, LaSalle, Dimmit and Zapata.

By 1914, business blossomed and the partners sought a downtown location, moving across from the Hamilton Hotel, selling Fords, Cadillacs, Overland Willises and Dodges. They opened a Ford garage on Jarvis Plaza. During World War I, Ford asked LAS for exclusive representation. Crates of Model T parts stacked up in the warehouse by the tracks. When the war ended, LAS was able to put Doughboys to work instantly and soon expanded with dealerships in Encinal, Hebbronville, Mirando City and Alice.

In 1925, Sames and Moore divided their partnership. Sames took the automotive enterprise and Moore the wholesale enterprise. W. J. Sames became company president, and sons Harry E. and W. J., Jr., were vice-president and secretary/sales manager, respectively. A new dealership was built at the corner of Houston and Convent.

W. J. Sr. died in 1940. The sons divided the companies and Harry bought out his mother's interests. Harry Sr. died in 1955 and was succeeded by his son, Harry E. Sames, Jr., and his grandson, Harry E. "Hank" Sames, III, who manages the firm today.

Progress took the latter Harry's to their present location where they sell Fords, Lincolns, Mercurys, Hondas, and Mazdas. This four-generation dealership now employs 200 people and sells over 4,000 new and used cars annually.

Sames Motor Company is proud of its stature as Texas' Oldest dealership.

Sames Motor Company is located at 6001 San Dario, Laredo, Texas 78041, 956-721-4700.

Top: Original Laredo Auto Sales Company in 1910 in downtown Laredo.

Below: W. J. Sames, co-founder of Laredo Auto Sales, 1910, and founder of Sames Motor Company, 1925.

Pelican's Wharf

Pelican's Wharf has been a landmark and dining tradition since its founding in 1981. A full-service restaurant and bar, it features quality seafood and steaks along with a varied selection of delicious entrees and appetizers. The bar opens daily with a "happy hour" from five to eight. Wine list and liquor selections range from affordable tothe most discriminating tastes.

Current owners, Mille Theis and George Martinez have played critical roles in creating such a well received restaurant and lounge. Both began waiting tables at the restaurant when it opened. Within three months, Theis was promoted to manager. Within six months, she was an operating partner. In 1986, Theis and Martinez, along with the Herring Group, purchased the restaurant from Pelican's Wharf, Inc. The Herring Group sold their interests to a silent partner in 1990. Successful management has twice won Theis the award of Laredo Restaurateur of the Year, in 1988 and 1996.

Martinez was promoted to headwaiter and within a year was the manager in charge of maintaining quality control in the kitchen. Martinez is no longer involved in the day-to-day operation of the restaurant, leaving in 1994 to pursue other interests.

With revenues well over $1 million annually, Pelican's Wharf boasts an employee roster of 44, many of whom have been with the establishment for over 10 years. Pelican's Wharf has been a training ground for many of Laredo's youth, allowing them to work while completing high school or college. Tuition assistance is made available to qualifying employees.

"We're proud of the hundreds of youths who have come here for their first job," said Theis. "We enable them to stay in school. We work around their school schedules so they don't work too many hours."

Noted for its community involvement, Pelican's Wharf frequently donates in-kind services for many organizations.

Pelican's Wharf is located at 4119 San Dario Avenue, Laredo, Texas 78041, 956-727-5070.

UNITED INDEPENDENT SCHOOL DISTRICT

In the spring of 1961, trustees from three tiny common school districts in Webb County met to consolidate—Cactus (later renamed Bilbo), on the Callaghan Ranch, Johnson (later renamed Masterson), on the Zapata Highway, and Nye, originally located on the south end of Santa Maria Avenue. Two other schools had already merged with Cactus—Webb in 1945 and Prairie View in 1959. The 1961-62 school year was the first for UISD, with 341 students in grades one through nine.

UISD gained national attention in the fall of 1963, when the first underground school in the nation opened with grades six through eleven. Underground classrooms were designed to double as community shelters in the event of an atomic war and served as a model for over 300 schools across the nation. The school received a citation from the Department of Defense.

The district made headlines again in 1964. At a time when state law prohibited students from speaking Spanish at school, trustees and administration met with Texas Education Agency officials and University of Texas foreign language professors to design and implement a bilingual education program in the first grade. UISD was one of the first districts in the nation to teach the Spanish-speaker English and the English-speaker Spanish. For the first time, border students were permitted to speak their native language on school grounds. UISD has remained an innovator and a leader in curriculum development.

UISD comprises north and southwest Laredo, including all of the growth areas of the city, as well as 75 percent of Webb County, covering 2,448 square miles. UISD is one of the fastest growing school districts in Texas. The 1999-00 student population was over 25,000 in grades pre-kindergarten through twelfth. UISD has three high schools, a health science magnet program, a business magnet program, an alternative school, 7 middle schools and 21 elementary schools. UISD voters passed a $115 million bond election in 1998. The bond money is expected to cover construction costs over the next five years of growth based on current projections. Construction projects will include ten new schools, school additions, renovations, traffic improvement projects, instructional technology, and a student activity complex/education center.

✧

Top: UISD Superintendent, Dr. R. Jerry Barber, reads to Perez Elementary School students during Children's Book Week.

Below: Finley Elementary School teachers and staff are proud that their campus was named a National Blue Ribbon School by the U.S. Department of Education. Finley is the first Laredo school to receive this highly distinguished honor.

Reliant Energy Entex

For nearly a century, Reliant Energy Entex and its predecessor companies have supplied the City of Laredo with dependable natural gas service.

Natural gas development began in 1910, in the old Randado field, some 22 miles from Laredo. The Reiser brothers struck gas sand while attempting to drill a deep artesian water well. The well was completed as a gas well.

Dr. M. P. Cullinan organized the Border Gas Company, later acquired by a predecessor of United Gas. Gas was piped for distribution into the City of Laredo, then a town of 14,000 in population. Laredo was one of the first four or five towns in the state of Texas to enjoy the advantages of natural gas.

In 1946, the Laredo District was set up in United Gas' Southwest Texas Division, serving seven Texas towns and Nuevo Laredo, Mexico.

United Gas merged with Pennzoil in 1968. Two years later, the distribution unit was spun off as United Gas, Inc. In 1974, the name was changed to Entex, Inc. In 1976, Entex acquired the distribution properties of Houston Natural Gas Corporation. Then, in 1988, Entex divested its remaining non-distribution assets and merged with NorAm and, in 1997, merged with Reliant Energy, formerly known as Houston Industries, becoming one of the top five combination gas and electric companies in the nation.

Today, the Laredo office serves as headquarters for the Laredo District and is home to 35 employees. Reliant Energy Entex has kept up as Laredo has grown. With approximately 371-miles of main lines and 167-miles of service lines, Reliant Energy Entex continually extends lines to serve new residential, commercial, and industrial customers.

Reliant Energy Entex is also keeping up with new technology and is providing natural gas service to the City of Laredo's El Metro municipal transit system for the compressed natural gas refueling station that opened in July, 1995. Texas A&M International University has also enjoyed the efficient economical advantages of natural gas since 1995.

✧

Top: Reliant Energy Entex had been headquartered at 903 Hidalgo since its beginning.

Below: Reliant Energy Entex relocated to its new facility at 1901 Market Street in July, 1999.

La India Packing Company, Inc.

Left: *La India Packing Company founder Antonio Rodriguez and his wife Antonia.*

Below: *Current La India owner and President Mrs. Lupita Rodriguez.*

Bottom: *Youngest son, Ruben Rodriguez (deceased), displaying their Mexican chocolate.*

For 76 years life has been spicy for Antonio Rodriguez and his descendants. Don Antonio started his business by making and selling *piruli*, a Mexican candy. He and his wife, Antonia Villarreal Rodriguez, opened La India Packing Company, Inc. in 1923, selling sundries and Mexican chocolate from their small grocery located in a little house on Marcella Avenue.

Don Antonio delivered his products via bicycle and Doña Antonia helped by grinding *cacao* by hand, from which he made his delicious hot chocolate drink, which is still very popular. Eventually Mexican spices were included in the inventory from which he creatively blended his famous *chorizo* and *menudo* mixes.

"Later on my grandfather decided to sell only spices, seasonings and herbs," said Elsa Sanchez, current La India general manager, secretary and treasurer. "By this time he had started to lose his sight and eventually became blind, but he never stopped working."

Upon Don Antonio's death, the Rodriguez' children, Oscar, Maria Luisa, Hector, Romeo, Ruben and Hilda, inherited the business. In 1990, Lupita Rodriguez, widow of Ruben, purchased the business from her in-laws. Elsa has taken the business from completely manual to automated.

The natural, quality products have filled a niche in this border city and beyond, enjoying popularity in Houston, Dallas, Austin, Fort Worth, the Rio Grande Valley and in Oklahoma. Elsa is planning to create distribution points in all areas of the U.S. with large pockets of Hispanic customers.

The business now has 14 employees and has introduced new products to the expanding ethnic market, including Tejano seasoning, orange pepper and Pica Rico seasonings for fruits, vegetables, snacks and miscellaneous health products.

A small on-site teahouse features teas, coffees and Don Antonio's famous hot Mexican chocolate along with finger sandwiches and other tea time foods.

La India Packing Company, Inc. is still located at 1520 Marcella Avenue, Laredo, Texas 78040; (956) 723-3772.

Laredo Independent School District

Public education in Texas was founded in Laredo on March 22, 1783, when the town council obeyed a royal decree that children up to the age of 12 were to learn to read and write and be taught Christian doctrine.

Nearly a hundred years later, on June 29, 1882, the Laredo City Council formulated the Laredo Independent School District in response to a petition raised by 20 citizens asking the city council to assume control of the public free schools in Laredo. Captain Edward R. Tarver was appointed the first superintendent at an annual salary of $750. From 1887-1901, H. G. Dickinson, Foxhall Parker, Louis D. Antin, Charles Pierce, and B. F. Pettus guided the district, followed by Louis J. Christen (1901-29); William P. Galligan (1929-46); J. W. Nixon (1946-73); Vidal Treviño (1973-95); Graciela Ramirez (1995-98); and Dr. Paul A. Cruz (1998-present).

A committee of City Council aldermen appointed by the mayor, served as the executive school board from 1882 until 1899. At that time, a seven-member school board was elected.

Over a hundred years after its founding, Laredo ISD has evolved from a one-room school system to a 30-campus district that served over 24,000 students in 1999, maturing into one of the best districts in the state for its size and resources. Always an educational innovator, the district established instructional programs from early childhood centers to technological programs for students in all grade levels. The performing arts for local high school students were greatly enhanced with the establishment of the Vidal M. Treviño School of Communications and Fine Arts in 1994. A new health and science magnet school opened in 1999 at Martin High School.

Existing facilities are continually modernized and new ones constructed to accommodate students well into the 21st century and to provide LISD students with a stimulating and invigorating educational setting. Technology has taken center stage, preparing students for future educational endeavors and the world of work.

Top: Urbahn Elementary School was constructed in the early 1920's and is now part of the Vidal M. Treviño Magnet School in the historic St. Peter's district.

Below: Martin High School replaced old Laredo High in 1937. Old Laredo High School is now the La Posada Hotel.

La Posada Hotel/Suites

The La Posada Hotel is forever tied to Texas and Mexico. Rich in history and tradition, it stands on the Rio Grande where Don Tomas Sanchez chose to settle Villa de San Agustin de Laredo in 1755.

By 1790, Laredo, with over 700 citizens, had become a concentration point for royal Spanish troops. As Mexico challenged Spain for its independence, Laredo assumed a pivotal role, with troops from both sides stationing themselves in the river community. By 1836, the Republic of Texas had stretched to the Rio Grande, including Laredo. Border cities joined several northern Mexico states in forming the short-lived Republic of the Rio Grande, seeking independence from both Mexico and Texas. It's capital was the present Republic of the Rio Grande Museum site, located on the La Posada's grounds.

The streets of Laredo remained rough and rustic until well into the 1920s, but Laredo's leaders recognized the value of educating its youth. In 1916, town leaders dedicated Laredo High School. Generations of citizens were educated at the plaza school.

In 1961, the old school was converted into the La Posada Hotel/Suites, welcoming guests from across the globe. The hotel's popularity has resulted in two expansions, encompassing structures on the east and west sides to create dining, lounging, ballroom, office, and meeting facilities.

In 1994, Barbara Fasken purchased the historic hotel and continues its operation through Palafox Hospitality, Ltd. A multi-million dollar renovation updated the decor and safety systems but left the historic architecture and ambiance intact. Almost 40 years after registering its first guest, the 208-room La Posada continues to reflect its Spanish heritage, maintain strong ties to the history and traditions of Texas and Mexico and take the state's lead in the development of North American free trade.

La Posada Hotel/Suites is located at 1000 Zaragoza Street; (956) 722-1701; www.laposadahotel-laredo.com

Laredo Convention & Visitors Bureau

As the official convention and visitor marketing entity for the City of Laredo, the Laredo Convention and Visitors Bureau (LCVB) mission is to enhance the Laredo area economy by the creation of an ever increasing demand for the visitor related facilities and services located in and around the City of Laredo.

Laredo's position on the border of the United States and Mexico is its greatest single attraction. From its earliest days, Laredo has attracted visitors from both the north and the south. They come to shop and to enjoy Laredo's hotels, restaurants, and cultural, historic, and natural attractions. New and sophisticated healthcare facilities are attracting more and more persons in search of quality medical treatment.

Recognizing that heritage tourism has made travel the single largest industry in Europe, the LCVB emphasizes Laredo's abundance of historical sites, including four intact historical neighborhoods. Their street plans, featuring a plaza as the central element, provide immediate testimony to Laredo's 1755 Spanish roots.

Top: Heritage tourism based around Laredo's abundance of historical sites draws thousands of visitors to Laredo each year.

Right: Visitors from both north and south of the border come to Laredo for its shopping, hotels, healthcare facilities, and natural attractions.

Laredo is emerging as an important birding destination, with birdwatchers lured by such rare species as the white-collared seedeater, red-billed pigeon and gray crowned yellowthroat. Hundreds of species of birds and butterflies migrate through the area.

The City Council created the Convention and Visitors Bureau as a City department in 1994, to promote the City's visitor resources. Funded by hotel/motel occupancy tax, virtually the entire LCVB budget supports a comprehensive convention and visitor marketing program. The LCVB partners with tourism interests in Nuevo Laredo in mutually beneficial promotions.

Laredo has enormous potential as a destination for group tours and other visitors, as well as a venue for meetings, conventions, and trade shows, according to LCVB Director Don Raulie. He and the other members of the LCVB team are responsible for creating and implementing an aggressive marketing strategy to develop that potential.

Laredo Convention and Visitor's Bureau, 501 San Agustin Avenue, Laredo, Texas 78040; 956-795-2200.

Central Power and Light Company

Top: Central Power and Light Company entered this float in the Trades Division of the 1939 Washington's Birthday Celebration parade. Not a prizewinner, the float attracted much attention, nevertheless, with its clever employment of Reddy Kilowatt figures pointing out the many uses and conveniences of electricity.

PHOTO BY SHERITON BURR.

Below: The Laredo Central Power and Light Company Ice and Cold Storage plant and offices, circa 1930.

Few today have experience of living without electricity, taking for granted the delivery of such services at the flip of a switch. Almost a century ago, these services barely existed in South Texas.

Thomas Edison's discovery of an incandescent lighting system supported by central station generation dates from the 1870's, but only the nation's largest cities had efficient electric utility systems at the time America entered World War II. Cities like Laredo still had rudimentary electric power networks, often surviving financially only on the strength of a street lighting contract or a streetcar franchise. Smaller towns, if they had electricity at all, were "sundown to midnight" systems, operating only during the hours of darkness.

Municipal water systems were most often served by wells. If people had gas service, it was "manufactured" gas made by burning coal and capturing the gases that resulted. Without the utility services we have become so accustomed to, life was difficult.

In 1889, an electric trolley system was operated in Laredo, replacing mule-drawn streetcars. Laredo's was the first streetcar system west of the Mississippi River, operational a full year ahead of San Antonio's.

Central Power and Light's entry into the South Texas utility business in 1916 was spread across five services: electricity, electric street railway traction, gas, water, and ice. Those services were primitive compared to today.

In 1917, the construction of utility lines allowed service to customers from the company's most efficient generating units. These lines linked South Texas by the 1920's. CPL sold and financed electric appliances, which became standard equipment for South Texas homes after 1925.

Wars, floods, hurricanes, financial woes, and fuel diversification took their toll over the years, but CPL has flourished. Central Power and Light's commitment to customer service is the same today as it was in 1916—delivery of the most reliable, efficient and reasonably priced service.

Casso, Guerra & Company

Casso, Guerra & Company has carved a unique niche in Laredo's history, built upon an international foundation. In 1893, Raul Casso moved to Nuevo Laredo, Tamaulipas, Mexico, from his native Agualeguas, Nuevo Leon. In 1901, he married Arnulfa Guerra. Shortly after their marriage, he joined her family's firm, M. Guerra Hermanos, who, at the turn of the century, operated the largest retail general merchandise store in Nuevo Laredo. Arnulfa's brothers, Matias and Macedonio, owned the business.

In 1914, during the Mexican Revolution, the business burned down and the Casso and Guerra families immigrated to the United States. Upon their arrival in Laredo, each family opened separate retail stores. Raul Casso founded Raul Casso & Cia. In 1916, Raul invited his brothers-in-law to join him and Casso, Guerra & Company was founded. Raul, Arnulfa, and their three children, Raul, Jr., Alfonso, and Angelina, lived on the second floor above the business on the corner of Iturbide and Salinas Streets in downtown Laredo.

In the 1920s, due to the demand for goods from outlying farms and ranches, Casso, Guerra & Company began to wholesale food products and make deliveries. In 1939, the Guerra brothers left the business. Matias Guerra went on to become Governor of the State of Tamaulipas. After World War II, the expanding company moved to its present location at 310 Guadalupe Street.

In 1995, Casso, Guerra & Company returned to its roots by establishing a sister company, Casso, Guerra de Mexico, in Nuevo Laredo. With an emphasis still on wholesale grocery delivery, the company added a new venture—the packaging and distribution of pinto beans and rice under their own labels.

Today, the company continues to distribute American products on both sides of the border as well as import high quality Mexican products for distribution throughout the State of Texas. In addition to wholesale grocery sales to retail stores, bakeries, and food service accounts, the company also distributes ammunition and other firearm accessories and photographic film, papers, and chemicals from Kodak and Polaroid.

Casso, Guerra & Company is currently owned by Alfonso Casso, Alfonso Casso, Jr., Luis R. Casso, and Laura Casso.

Top: The original Casso, Guerra & Company on Salinas Avenue in downtown Laredo, circa 1919.

Below: The Guerra brother's store on Guerrero Street in Nuevo Laredo, Tamaulipas, circa 1900.

South Texas National Bank

South Texas National Bank was organized in 1977 and opened its doors for business in December. Over 20 years later, the bank has assets totaling over $260 million.

Original organizers were Ruben M. Garcia, Ray M. Keck, Jr., Harry E. Sames, Jr., Dean Sanditen, and Fernando F. Zuniga, Jr. Edward Starr served as the first bank president until 1978.

Three additional directors were elected to the board in 1978: Charles Alexander, Jr., George Link and Carroll E. Summers. Marion Bristow became the second president, serving until 1981.

Douglas G. Macdonald became STNB's third president in 1981 and still serves in that capacity. George J. Person and Evan J. Quiros were elected to the board of directors in 1982.

In 1984, STNB formed a one-bank holding company, Southshares, Inc., which bought the majority of the outstanding stock of South Texas National Bank. In 1992, Laredo National Bancshares, Inc. bought all the outstanding shares of Southshares, Inc., hence, Southshares ceased to exist and South Texas National Bank became a subsidiary of Laredo National Bancshares, Inc.

STNB currently has three locations, two in Laredo and one in Eagle Pass. The bank is planning to expand its holdings northward to Del Rio and southward to the Valley. "We're expanding along the Texas/ Mexico border, which is where this bank's expertise lies," said Macdonald.

The current board of directors includes Douglas Brice, Joaquin G. Cigarroa, III, Ike Epstein, Charles Farrell, Douglas G. Macdonald, George Person, Humberto Piña, Carroll E. Summers, James D. Walker, Fernando F. Zuniga, Jr., and O. Enrique Hinojosa Peña as advisory director.

STNB'S executive management consists of President Douglas Macdonald, Executive Vice President Rene Solis, Senior Vice President Yolanda P. Jiminez, Senior Vice President Jose I. Maldonado, Senior Vice President Roberto Mireles, and First Vice President and Cashier Judi R. Cruz.

In Laredo, STNB is located at 2211 Guadalupe and in Walker Plaza, 5810 San Bernardo Avenue, 956-724-8411.

✧

Top: South Texas National Bank facility at Walker Plaza, 5810 San Bernardo Avenue.

Below: South Texas National Bank facility at 2211 Guadalupe.

Ace Carton & Tape of Laredo, Inc.

✧

Josephine Benavides, co-owner of Ace Carton & Tape of Laredo, Inc., stands amid a display of some of the items the firm sells and distributes.

Oskar Benavides Vann, Sr. found his niche in life as an entrepreneur. In 1965, deciding to be the captain of his own fate, he founded Ace Carton & Tape Sales, Inc., in San Antonio. He and his wife, Josephine, based their enterprise on their knowledge of corrugated boxes and tapes.

The couple's son, Oskar, Jr., began his training in the family business at the age of 16. As the business grew, the family divided the company and installed a satellite office in Laredo, where Oskar, Jr. presides.

Ace Carton & Tape of Laredo, Inc. was created in 1980. As international trade expanded, the need for the company's products became more diverse, as did their customer base. Ace Carton & Tape of Laredo, Inc. developed business in all parts of Mexico, Central America and the Caribbean. Their Monterrey, Nuevo Leon, Mexico office sells and distributes to all points of the Republic of Mexico. The company is continually on the watch for ways to add value to their product base while maintaining the excellence of their workmanship and service.

Products offered by the company include: all sizes of corrugated boxes, in 200-pound and 350-pound test; packaging products such as poly tape, carton sealing tape, duct tape, electrical tape, colored tape, fiberglass reinforced tape, poly propylene strapping tape, packaging list protection tape, label protection tape, Kraft sealing tape, Kraft reinforced tape, masking tape, double coated tape, cloth tape and reflective tape; bubble film rolls; cushioning roll foam; tape dispensers; bin boxes; mailers, Kraft paper rolls; twist ties; floor sweep; stretch wrap; loose fill peanuts; and single face corrugation.

Ace Carton also stocks tools, including steel tensioners, steel crimpers, and cutters; steel banding; poly banding; seals; corner protectors; truck seals in aluminum, plastic, and metal; air bags; and industrial and king-sized permanent markers in a wide color assortment.

Ace Carton can create customized boxing and packaging materials, including the use of personal imprinting.

Ace Carton & Tape of Laredo, Inc., is located at 919 Santa Maria Avenue, P.O. Box 2745, Laredo, Texas 78044-2745.

Union Pacific Railroad

The coming of the railroad in 1881 changed Laredo forever. The Union Pacific rail line from San Antonio to Laredo was originally constructed by the International and Great Northern Railroad. It became part of the Missouri Pacific Railroad in 1873 and in 1982 merged with Union Pacific.

Union Pacific Railroad is a subsidiary of Union Pacific Corporation, a Fortune 500 company headquartered in Dallas, with regional operating offices spanning the nation. Union Pacific Corporation is the largest railroad in North America, operating in the western two-thirds of the U.S. The system serves 23 states, linking every major West Coast and Gulf Coast port.

Union Pacific is Texas' largest railroad, serving all of its major cities and gulf ports. With lines to the international gateways at El Paso, Laredo, Eagle Pass, and Brownsville, Union Pacific is the primary U.S. rail link to Mexico. In Texas, Union Pacific runs over 6,349 miles of track and employs over 8,700 persons with a $522.8 million payroll.

Laredo is Union Pacific's primary Mexico gateway, handling seventy to eighty-percent of its rail cargo into and out of Mexico. In addition to the railroad switchyard located in the downtown area, it operates Port Laredo, a major intermodal terminal and classification yard facility in North Laredo. Under construction since 1990 with a cost of $40 million, the 530-acre facility has been expanded with additional tracks and cranes to accommodate more than 800 trailers and 1,200 rail cars.

Major commodities shipped through the Laredo port include autos and auto parts, industrial products (metals, minerals and forest products), intermodal trailers and containers, agricultural products, and chemicals.

Union Pacific has a $1.5 million federal services building and inspection area at Port Laredo. The facility improves the inspection process for U.S. Customs Border Patrol and the Department of Agriculture. In addition, Union Pacific spent $9.2 million on track improvements and signal construction on the line between Laredo and San Antonio.

✧

Top: The International Railroad Bridge into Mexico.

Below: Union Pacific Railroad depot.

O.N.L.Y. Collections

When women of the world gather, one consistent topic of conversation is fashion. Laredo is no exception. Laredo's Limón family carries its love for fashionable clothing to another level as owners and managers of a smart, stylish boutique that caters to the whims of Laredo's most fashion conscious shopper. O.N.L.Y. Collections—a name devised from the first letter in the owners' names—Oralia, Norma, Lizette, and Yvonne—was created in 1994, when Norma decided it might be easier to open a boutique rather than appease the stylish desires of her three fashion conscious daughters. Joined in business by her daughters, they are making a good team.

Norma has years of history in the world of haute couture, having worked at several of Laredo's smartest clothing shops. She serves as a buyer and seller for O.N.L.Y. Collections, as do Oralia Limón Newton and Yvonne Limón Casso. Both daughters have studied fashion and merchandising. Lizette Limón serves as the boutique's manager, accountant, and marketing director.

The team selects pieces for their shop that serve as basic wardrobe builders, with strength in basic colors. Pizzazz is added through a careful selection of smashing designer pieces and accessories. The team selects clothing lines that complement each other and work well together.

Designer lines carried by O.N.L.Y. Collections include both domestic and imported fashion houses. The shop also carries a small line of lingerie. The small boutique caters to its clientele with personalized service. Clientele is largely local with a growing attention from out-of-town and country shoppers.

By all signs, the youngest female in the family, Oralia's daughter, Christian is planning to carry a fondness for fashion into the third generation.

O.N.L.Y. Collections is located in a shopping center at 101 West Hillside, Suite 4, Laredo, Texas 78041 956-791-6659.

The Limón family (left to right): Oralia Limón Newton, Norma Limón, Yvonne Limón Casso, Christian Newton, and Lizette Limón.

LAREDO DEVELOPMENT FOUNDATION

The Laredo Development Foundation, incorporated in 1966, serves Laredo, Webb County, Texas and Nuevo Laredo, Mexico. It is a private, non-profit corporation funded and governed by local business and civic leaders dedicated to the area's continued economic development. LDF's primary responsibility is to help create jobs.

With early encouragement by Carlton Whitworth of Central Power & Light, Max Mandel of Laredo National Bank, Honore Ligarde of International Bank of Commerce, and Byron Miller of Union National Bank decided that the private sector could help the area create jobs. In 1966, along with Laredo businessmen Robert Freeman, Tom Herring, J. C. Martin, Jr., G. R. Peck, Robert Pratt, J. J. Richter, Roberto Benavides, J. W. Kramer, Robert Trautmann, and W. L. Webber, they created LDF. Under the leadership of its 13 founders and 18 board presidents, LDF has worked hard for Laredo and Nuevo Laredo, establishing a proud record of integrity, performance, and service.

Completely reorganized in 1980, LDF became a full-time, professionally staffed organization with city and county funding as well as private sector support. The organization has become heavily involved in attracting new industry, helping local businesses start up and expand, preparing economic studies to support local project priorities and conducting an outreach program on environmental awareness and hazmat accident prevention.

LDF activities are structured under four operating divisions and one internal division: industrial attraction, small business development, environmental protection, special projects and administration.

Since its inception, LDF has helped create over 11,000 new Laredo jobs in a variety of businesses, including manufacturing, trade, transportation, distribution, and retail. In addition, over 20,000 jobs have been created in Nuevo Laredo maquiladora plants. These 100 plants have 25 twin plant operations in Laredo, accounting for 3,000 jobs. Very few Laredo business location decisions are made without LDF data and assistance.

Recent census data shows Laredo as the fastest growing city in Texas and second fastest in the nation. Economic indicators show that the economy is more than keeping up with population growth. Employment levels, new business starts and new housing starts continue to increase as unemployment decreases.

Since 1990, LDF's Small Business Development Division has operated a Small Business Administration-sponsored development center to provide counseling and management training assistance to new business ventures. The center's success has been remarkable, whereas 250 center clients have obtained $75 million in SBA-guaranteed loans for new businesses with 5,000 new jobs created for Laredo.

Front row (from left to right): Araceli E. Lozano, John A. Adams, Jr., and Isabel Salazar. Back row: Gladys Rangel, Laura Cantu, Yvette Medina, Lily Torres, and Rena Villa.

LDF is considered by industry professionals to be the best team of economic developers on the border. Foundation administration has been able to recruit and train highly motivated, hard working professionals who believe in what they do. All LDF staff members are trained in their respective specialties and are cross-trained to assist with other activities. Courses required for LDF staff include industrial location theory, business retention and expansion, project financing, prospect handling, land use, real estate principles, foreign trade zones, targeting techniques, international trade, business plans, economic impact analysis, and transportation and labor issues, among others.

The Texas-Mexican Railway Company

Before 1848, travelers across south Texas had to ride on horseback, use a wagon or go around by riverboat. Stagecoach travel was often dangerous. Passengers had to contend with heat, dust, long rides, and Indians or bandit attacks. As populations increased, faster mail and passenger service was needed.

In 1866, Uriah Lott arrived in South Texas building over 1,400 miles of track in his lifetime. In 1877, Lott began laying track to Laredo from Corpus Christi, encountering less than avid enthusiasm from Laredo businessmen who were aware that two other railroads were also approaching. The Palmer-Sullivan syndicate had negotiated with Mexico to construct a narrow-gauge railroad, the Mexican National, that would run from Mexico City, and Jay Gould's International & Great Northern was approaching from San Antonio.

In 1881, Lott met with General William Jackson Palmer, who surmised that Lott's tracks could provide him with an immediate outlet to the Gulf. He bought the line and immediately incorporated as The Texas-Mexican Railway. Work on the railway was completed that year.

In 1890, Tex-Mex moved its main offices and shop facilities from Corpus to Laredo. At the time, the shops were the largest engine facilities west of the Mississippi, accommodating up to 40 locomotives.

Initially, all steam engines used by Tex-Mex were fueled with hot-burning mesquite wood. In 1906, the company turned to coal. New engines purchased in 1920 used fuel oil. Tex-Mex was the first large railroad in the nation to convert completely to diesel in 1938. Piggyback service was inaugurated during the 1950s to carry freight packed in trailers.

In 1982, Transportacion Maritima Mexicana, an international freight-forwarding and steamship line, purchased Tex-Mex, and in 1995, sold 49 percent of the company to Kansas City Southern Industries.

Tex-Mex is developing plans to construct a new 14-track, 1,600 car-capacity yard at Laredo and an intermodal facility to handle double-stack units for between 1,200 and 1,500 trucks per day.